J. RICHARD GENTRY

W9-BPM-599

Breakthrough in
Beginning Reading
and Writing

The Evidence-Based Approach to Pinpointing
Students' Needs and Delivering Targeted Instruction

■SCHOLASTIC

NEW YORK • TORONTO • LONDON • AUCKLAND • SYDNEY
MEXICO CITY • NEW DELHI • HONG KONG • BUENOS AIRES

Dedication

For all teachers

especially for six who changed my life

Bonnie Wright Gentry—my mother and first-grade teacher

Mary Alice Elliot—my high school history teacher

Bruce Cobbs—Elementary Education, University of North Carolina, Chapel Hill

And in memory of

Thomas O. Gentry—my uncle, Scout Master, and eighth-grade teacher

Edmund H. Henderson—Graduate Reading Education, The University of Virginia

Marie M. Clay—for her extraordinary contributions to beginning reading education

∷

The author and publisher wish to thank those who have generously given permission to reprint material:
Figures 1.2, 1.3, and 2.4 from *Nursery Rhyme Time: Reading and Learning Sounds, Letters and Words* by J. Richard Gentry and Richard S. Craddock. Copyright © 2005 by Universal Publishing. Reprinted by permission.
Figure 8.1 from *Overcoming Dyslexia* by Sally Shaywitz. Copyright © 2003 by Knopf. Reprinted by permission.

Scholastic grants teachers permission to photocopy the reproducible pages from this book for classroom use. No other part of this publication may be reproduced in whole or in part, or stored in a retrieval system, or transmitted in any form or by any means, electronic, mechanical, photocopying, recording, or otherwise, without permission of the publisher. For information regarding permission, write to Scholastic Inc., 557 Broadway, New York, NY 10012.

Editor: Lois Bridges
Production editor: Amy Rowe
Cover designer: Maria Lilja
Interior designer: Sarah Morrow
Copy editor: Shea Dean

ISBN-13: 978-0-545-00725-2
ISBN-10: 0-545-00725-9
Copyright © 2007 by J. Richard Gentry
All rights reserved. Published by Scholastic Inc.
Printed in the U.S.A.

1 2 3 4 5 6 7 8 9 10   40   13 12 11 10 09 08 07

Table of Contents

::

Acknowledgments

This book reflects the brilliance, patient reflection, and loving care of my gentle editor, Lois Bridges. I came to Lois with the concept for this book with trepidation, and she did for me what great teachers do for children—she believed in me, gave me inspiration, pushed me to higher accomplishment, and rescued me when I was faltering. How fortunate I am to have been shepherded by this insightful editor and lovely person, who not only brings to bear a doctorate in education and special command of language and literacy issues, but who also has worked with so many outstanding authors who write for teachers. It is an enriching personal and professional experience and an honor to work with Lois Bridges. My admiration, respect, and appreciation for her guidance and inspiration are forever and enduring.

I acknowledge with warm appreciation the assistance of a spectacular staff at Scholastic. A special thank you to Terry Cooper as a team builder and collaborator whose insights have benefited this book. I wish to thank Amy Rowe for untiring devotion as production editor and her cheerful, gracious, skillful work. Ray Coutu steered this work in the right direction, and Shea Dean's smart, meticulous, and reflective copy editing were a precious gift making this a stronger book. I am grateful to Susan Kolwicz, marketing manager extraordinaire, and Jaime Lucero, talented art director; my thanks also to Maria Lilja for the cover design and Sarah Morrow for the interior design.

A special thank you to Gloria Pipkin and Sandra Wilde for especially helpful guidance on early formulations of this work. I am grateful for their knowledge and friendship.

I have had the privilege of friendship and continuous dialogue on education with Bill McIntyre for nearly twenty years. His insightful contributions were enormously helpful in sections of this volume. I am indebted today to many educators, mentors, and special friends, such as Rosemarie Jensen for her generous dialogue and friendship. I also thank those from years past, such as mentor Ida Hathaway. In between there are so many others: Richard Craddock, Karl Studt, Judy Farley, Penny Jamiason, Lilia Nanez, Dalia Benavides, Patricia Baxter, Kristen Sousa, Jane Cooke, Paula Eggleston, Carolyn Meigs, Lester Laminack, Jean Mann, Charlene Kalinski, Cecilia Aitken, Linda Kidd, Peggy Sherman, Beverly Kingery, Paula Paulos, Cindy Jackson, Jeanette Maxwell, Kim McAbee, Kathy Vickio, and all who have contributed to my understanding of the meaning of education and how best to help children become successful readers and writers.

I am deeply indebted to a number of children and parents with whom I have worked over the years, who shared samples of work, many presented in this volume. Children's writings are my data, and without them I could not have learned about beginning reading or written this book. A special thank you to Annie Zimmer and Carrie Amon as well as the splendid faculty and staff at Mamaroneck Avenue School, and most especially to Albert, Sheily, Aileen, Kevin, Rossina, and Uma for inviting me to sit next to them and learn from them and with them. A special thank you to children whose personal journeys to literacy enlightened my own: Dan, Meredith, Leslie, Daniella, Michael, Ricky, Sarah, Britanny, Connor, and so many others. And thank you to Bill Miller, who shot and developed our terrific video footage.

In a book that seeks to show compatibility among disparate stances, I present the names of scholars side-by-side, many of whom have disputed each others' works. I am indebted to all of them for insightful contributions, most especially Linnea Ehri, Marie Clay, Yetta and Ken Goodman, Marilyn Adams, Regie Routman, Patrick McCabe, Tim Shanahan, Don Graves, Nancie Atwell, Stephanie Harvey, Lucy Calkins, Mary Jo Fresch, Charles Read, David Pearson, Dorothy Strickland, Elizabeth Sulzby, Richard Allington, Anne McGill-Franzen, Connie Juel, Pat Cunningham, Tim Rasinski, Catherine Snow, Sally Shaywitz, Keith Stanovich, Howard Margolis, Frank Smith, Isabell Cardonick, Eileen Feldgus, Shane Templeton, Darrell Morris, Jean Gillet, Jerry Zutell, Charlie Temple, Diane Snowball, Don Holdaway, Irene Fountas, Gay Su Pinnell, Maryann Manning, and so many others. We must all band together to better understand how to teach children to read.

Finally, I am most grateful to my loving family, most especially Bill Boswell for continuing support, caring, and happiness.

Preface

Breakthrough in Beginning Reading and Writing—for teachers, administrators, teacher educators, literacy coaches, parents, and educational researchers—outlines a new way of observing and supporting beginning reading and writing instruction. It provides a framework based on observation of each child's passage through meaningful and natural evidence-based phases of code breaking and uses phase observation to suggest effective strategies for teaching beginning literacy. In a tempered explanation of science and practice, Breakthrough in Beginning Reading and Writing demonstrates the compatibility of meaning-based and phonics-first theories of beginning reading. I believe knowledgeable teachers of beginning reading have always integrated phonics and meaning into their teaching. This book demonstrates how to integrate them in ways that are evidence-based and effective.

Breakthrough in Beginning Reading and Writing is a step in developing successful theory and practice that encompasses both meaning-first and phonics-first principles with scientifically grounded classroom instruction. It emphasizes sound instruction by teachers, who are empowered to make decisions and supported by appropriate curricular resources, professional development, and respect for the profession. The techniques and strategies suggested in this book are built upon the empirical investigations of scholars from both meaning-based and code-emphasis perspectives. It is my hope that this text, which attempts to draw together the best of both perspectives and demonstrate their compatibility, will prompt a breakthrough to a new vision for teaching beginning reading and writing.

Introduction

When I entered the field of reading education more than thirty years ago, I was struck by the vagaries and mysteries of how to teach beginning reading. Like too many elementary education graduates today, I found it baffling. Thus, when I won my first teaching assignment, in a third-grade classroom, I had virtually no knowledge whatsoever of how to teach beginning reading. I didn't know about phase theory, which outlines an ordered, step-by-step, natural sequence of operations all beginning readers and writers employ (Ehri, 1997; Gentry, 2006), and I found myself facing Alan, who was essentially a nonreader. I mustered the courage to approach our school's powerful and much feared resource teacher, Mrs. Hathaway, and reported my dilemma: "Mrs. Hathaway, I don't know how to teach beginning reading. What am I supposed to do with Alan?"

For the next six months, Mrs. Hathaway came into my classroom every day to work with Alan and lead my struggling reading group, and she helped me understand some of the nuances of beginning reading. It was a trial-and-error learning process on a road filled with land mines for both the children and me, but Alan and the two other little guys in my low reading group made progress. Today I can tell you, a teacher's first experiences with beginning reading instruction do not have to be that way, and neither do the children's. Phase theory provides one clear path to teaching and learning beginning reading.

Major new findings in reading education and brain research that help dispel the confusion surrounding how to teach beginning reading are the subject of this book. One major new finding is that the little ones, beginning readers, are *different* from mature, skilled readers. For more than a hundred years, reading educators have treated little and big readers as though they were following the same reading process. More precisely, much of our beginning reading theory has assumed that the reading a beginner does is a reductionist version of the skilled reading that advanced readers do. Some of us believed the little ones—if we just waited—would grow naturally into accomplished readers. So either we waited for them to blossom into readers or, if they didn't, we identified them as *learning disabled*, most often between the ages of 11 and 17 (Gorman, 2003), and by then our intervention was too late and often ineffective.

What phase theory and the chapters ahead illuminate is that beginning readers aren't just little versions of skilled adult readers. Beginning readers are like tadpoles in metamorphosis, a metaphor I used in *Breaking the Code* (2006), and as with tadpoles and frogs, little readers are not smaller, developing versions of the mature ones. They are *different* versions, needing special nurturing, alternative environments, and unique kinds of instructional support for growth.

Educators often speak of "emerging readers" and "proficient readers" as if the emerging one is the same as the one it eventually grows into. The development of a tadpole into a frog doesn't work that way, and neither does proficient reading. There are no "emerging frogs," "low-progress frogs," "slow frogs," or frogs in some state of limbo waiting for social, emotional, and fine motor development, as well as left or right dominance, so that they can finally embrace froghood. Tadpoles are never "not ready" to become frogs. The same can be said for reading in spite of decades of confusion along these lines.

Beginning readers and skilled readers are not the same. We will learn that an important implication of this understanding is that we should joyfully place books in the hands of children from infancy onward and follow soon with writing tools and paper. *There is no need to wait!*

Brain scans provide good support for the notion that tadpole readers and frog readers are not the same. What beginning readers do neurologically, many in the first two years of schooling, may differ significantly from what's happening right now in your brain as you process the information on this page. The beginning reader's brain may activate different circuitry in different areas from yours, firing off different constellations of neurons. The beginning processes are slow and analytical and involve a great deal of imitation and repetition. The automatic, express pathway of mature reading activates later and involves a different area and different processing (Shaywitz, 2003). Even as breaking the code— understanding that letters and sounds are related—is foundational, it is fundamentally true that meaning is important from the very beginning.

What does phase theory mean for beginning reading instruction?

Phase theory instruction means that children experience the following:

- Meaningful writing of their own thoughts and feelings as a major entry point to reading

- Exposure to wonderful children's literature through read-alouds and book talks for building interest and motivation

- Academic vocabulary, sense of story, and enjoyment and appreciation of reading

- Joyful work with nursery rhymes and poems with lots of word play and singing

- Repetition and memorization for early reading

- Changes in focus of attention from one phase to the next

- Developmental growth from one phase to the next, gradually increasing knowledge of letters, graphemes, phonemes, graphophonemic associations, phonological/phonemic awareness, phonological recoding, spelling patterns, and lexicon of sight words stored in memory

At the foundation of reading, children must eventually recognize chunks of phonics patterns and more than one hundred high-frequency, one-syllable sight words to activate express pathways for reading (Gentry, 2006; Shaywitz, 2003). This book is designed to help you easily grasp this revolutionary new understanding. During most children's first two years of schooling, the "reading" they do is very different from the reading you do as your eyes skip across this page. Beginners imitate and memorize, ponder slowly and analytically, activate different brain areas, use different foci of attention, and need different instructional environments and support than mature readers do.

The seemingly insurmountable exigencies of teaching beginning reading have spanned the vast majority of my thirty-something-year teaching career. When I entered the doctoral program in reading education at the University of Virginia, Professor Edmund H. Henderson read aloud from the classic work of Edmund B. Huey. While it was written some sixty years prior to my arrival, it was, at the time, considered illuminating and akin to Albert Einstein's early writings on relativity—theoretically brilliant and groundbreaking.

Here's the passage Professor Henderson read out loud in the first class of my doctoral program. It is still marked in my copy of Huey's book from the night Professor Henderson read it:

> *And so to completely analyze what we do when we read would almost be the acme of a psychologist's achievements, for it would be to describe very many of the most intricate workings of the human mind, as well as to unravel the tangled story of the most remarkable specific performance that civilization has learned in all of its history.*
>
> (Huey, 1908, p. 6)

Breakthrough in Beginning Reading and Writing will help you unravel part of the "tangled story" of beginning reading as you consider some of the "most intricate workings of the human mind." The aspects highlighted will be those specifically related to breaking the code because these are foundational for learning to read and fundamentally misunderstood. You'll come to understand phase theory and learn how to get things right with code breaking.

A Note about the DVD: Watch Richard Gentry Conduct Literacy Interviews, Phase Analysis, and Placement

After reading Part I of *Breakthrough in Beginning Reading and Writing*, which presents a developmental snapshot of the five phases of code breaking, you may wish to review the phases in action on camera. The DVD accompanying this book shows me conducting literacy interviews with an analysis of six children whom I meet for the first time on camera. Once you see these engaging interactions, I will provide an explanation of how phase theory informs my analysis of each child's literacy development. You will see children, ages 4 to 6 years old, who clearly operate in different phases, providing an overview of phase theory. When you slide the DVD into your computer or DVD player, a menu will pop open on your screen with four sections. Let me briefly explain the offerings of each section.

1. Introduction

I share a brief overview of phase theory and explain its significance in helping you track and monitor your students' literacy development. I also explain options for using the DVD. You might prefer to read the book first and then watch the DVD; or you can watch the DVD first and then read the book; or you can alternate back and forth. Let your own needs and interests guide you.

2. Phase Overview

In this section, you'll see me conducting "literacy interviews" with six children who reflect four phases of development, Phases 1 through 4 (none of the children were Phase 0). I'll show you how to interact with children through conversations about and demonstrations of their reading and writing and, in the process, how to quickly discern where they fall on the developmental phase continuum.

3. Analysis

Once I've completed my student-by-student work with the six children, I line up the reading and writing assessment data I've collected during my literacy interviews with each child—from beginning phase to most sophisticated—and provide you with a quick overview of how I make my determinations regarding phase placement and why placement is so important. I also touch upon instructional follow-through for each child, demonstrating how knowledge of the child's phase shapes and guides instruction.

4. Conclusion

A quick wrap-up includes closing thoughts about the significance of phase theory for beginning reading and writing instruction.

PART I

The Five Phases of Code-Breaking

A Developmental Snapshot

....

If you can recognize a child's phase, you can pinpoint the child's needs and deliver targeted instruction. As soon as you identify the child's phase of development, you will have a complete picture of what he or she likely knows and does not know. The next five chapters focus simultaneously on reading and writing as we zero in on each phase, beginning with Phase 0, and review reasonable expectations for the phase, target the methods that focus on what the child is likely paying attention to as a reader and writer, and demonstrate how specific teaching methods help the child move to the next phase. For each phase, you will match specific instructional methods with specified goals for moving the child forward.

The chapters include charts summarizing the goals and major techniques for each phase. As we move through the phases, illustrative vignettes will help us see how identifying the child's phase greatly enhances our view of his or her reading and writing capabilities and expectations based on what he or she knows, is expected to know, and is paying attention to as a reader and a writer. In the material that follows, you will see vivid portraits of Corey, Dan, Leslie, and others that will make phase theory and the data it delivers accessible for practical classroom application.

CHAPTER 1

Phase 0: Operations Without Letter Knowledge

Phase 0

Key Operations

The child:

- Scribbles
- Cannot write his/her name
- Cannot invent a spelling

Critical Aspect

- Operations without letters

Systemic Goals

- Building interest and confidence in reading
- Instilling or fulfilling the child's urge to write
- Engaging the child in the reading and writing *system* by modeling reading and writing and by interacting with the child in reading and writing
- Attending to using the parts of reading and writing by directing the child's attention and focusing on the particular parts that are important for Phase 0
- Developing awareness of phonology appropriate for Phase 0
- Establishing explicit, phase-appropriate goals for language-specific knowledge
  - : Sounds
  - : Letters
  - : Book concepts

Practical Applications and Explicit Goals for Phase 0

- : Learning to recognize one's own name
- : Learning to read one's own name
- : Learning to write one's own name

Expectations for a Phase 0 Writer

- May know that writing is meaningful
- May have little understanding of how writing works
- May not know how to hold a pencil or pen
- May not know how to position the paper
- May not know how to orient print on the page
- Attempts are nonalphabetic
- Not yet able to write one's own name

- May already enjoy books
- May have developed some book-handling concepts

Practical Application and Explicit Goals for Phase 0

: Book orientation

: Page-turning

: Directionality

: May approximate reading

: May expect books to be meaningful

Expectations for Sound Knowledge at Phase 0

- Phonological Awareness

Practical Application and Explicit Goals for Phase 0

: May begin to clap out syllables in names

: May begin to shout out or otherwise designate rhyming words

: May begin to isolate beginning sound of his or her name

A Phase 0 Vignette: A First Glimpse of Developing Literacy

It takes me three seconds to know that Corey, who will turn four years old in a couple of weeks, is Phase 0. I ask her if she can write her name and she tells me she can't. The power of phase theory is that this seemingly small revelation is packed with information. Pinpointing the child's phase is a snapshot of where this child is developmentally, and the snapshot is loaded with data. If I confirm that Corey is indeed Phase 0, it's quite probable that she doesn't know letters and hasn't had a great deal of experience developing awareness of sounds such as rhyming words. I wonder about her book experience, and I can predict that she isn't reading a lot from memory. I wonder about her level of vocabulary development. Vocabulary development is an important consideration because, as reported by Betty Hart and Todd R. Rinsley, child psychologists and researchers at the University of Kansas whose landmark study followed 42 children from 10 months to age 3 with monthly home visits, it's probable that vocabulary growth may be much lower in children from disadvantaged homes—who are less likely to know their letters—than in children of professionals. In Hart and Rinsley's study, three-year-old children of professionals had vocabularies of about 1,100 words as compared with 525-word vocabularies possessed by welfare children (Tough, 2006). Even though I'm not concerned about Corey's economic status, the fact that she can't write her name makes me wonder if she has had lots of language exposure in early childhood. Thinking about her oral language experience may be important because language exposure has high correlations with her later academic success (Tough, 2006). As I think about Corey in light of phase theory, these are my hypotheses, and they help me to focus my attention on what's important for the child at this phase and to eliminate other considerations. If she can't write her name, there are a lot of other things I know that she can't do. If she can write her name, she's at Phase 1, encapsulating a more sophisticated set of capabilities and expectations.

My next step is to find out more about Corey by a second simple assessment. I might survey several samples of her "writing" so that I can see if she invents spellings and, if so, analyze them, or I might ask Corey to spell five words that have special sound features that will enable me to match her with a phase by analyzing the spelling. The Monster Test, which I first published in 1985, is the spelling option, and it's a quick and easy way to identify her phase level (Gentry, 1985; 2007a). I give Corey the first three words—*monster, united,* and *dress.* If she can't write her own name, I certainly don't expect her to invent spellings for these words, and my prediction is confirmed as I watch Corey make a single straight line from left to right across the page each time I ask her to write one of the words: *monster, united, dress.* This straight-line drawing is like more typical "wavy writing," "loopy writing," or squiggles. And interestingly, when I attempt to demonstrate "wavy writing," Corey ignores my request to try wavy lines in place of her straight lines, choosing to stick with what seems comfortable for her. I reassure Corey that her straight line writings are perfectly fine and suggest that I would like to help her write her name.

Corey is interested and quite agreeable with the name-writing suggestion, and I say, "Watch as I write your name, Corey, with this red marker. 'C'—here's the C. Did you know that your name begins with the letter, C? Here's the *o, r, e, y*. There it is, *Corey!* Can you read it?"

As I model each letter, I speak the sentence "Here's the *c, o, r, e, y*" slowly, with my articulation of the name of the letter matching the letter as I write it on the page. As I designate each letter, Corey experiences left-to-right directionality. The name-writing activity is teaching Corey the *system* of writing and reading, not simply a word. When I ask Corey if she can read her name, she says that she can.

Gentry: What does it say? [*Pointing to the word I have just written*]

Corey: Corey.

Gentry: Wow, that's great! You can read your own name!

Next I ask her if she can understand the letters and she shakes her head, indicating that she cannot, so I help her with them.

Gentry: Say the names of the letters as I point to them. This first one is C.

Corey: C.

Gentry: O.

Corey: O.

Gentry: R.

Corey: R.

Gentry: E.

Corey: E.

Gentry: Y.

Corey: Y.

Then I ask her to repeat it because I know that the brain loves repetition and that repetition will help Corey store in memory the names of the letters that spell her name.

Our next step is to have Corey trace the letters, and I bring out a darker pen so that she can trace over my red, two-inch letters. We position the paper as in Figure 1.2.

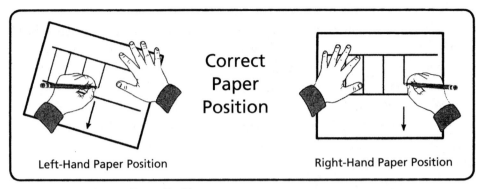

Correct Paper Position

Left-Hand Paper Position

Right-Hand Paper Position

FIGURE 1.2 Correct Paper Position

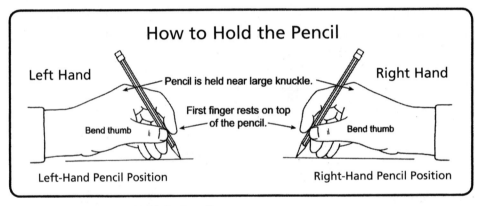

How to Hold the Pencil

Left Hand

Right Hand

Pencil is held near large knuckle.

First finger rests on top of the pencil.

Bend thumb

Bend thumb

Left-Hand Pencil Position

Right-Hand Pencil Position

FIGURE 1.3 How to Hold the Pencil

I'll watch to see if she knows how to hold a pencil, and if she doesn't grip it properly, I'll make an attempt to show her, following the model in Figure 1.3.

Corey may find this grip awkward at first, so I kind of go with the flow, readjusting the pencil position from time to time if I sense it will help her. I watch for pencil positioning, letter formation, and directionality. I'm getting a lot of detailed information regarding what she already knows and what I need to demonstrate or teach.

Corey is totally fascinated with our name tracing, and when we complete tracing her name for the first time she says, "Can I write it again?" This is a thrilling accomplishment because it indicates she's hooked. She's enjoying what we are doing, and she will be able to get the repetition that the brain needs—reading the name, writing the name, practicing the letters—to move to the next level.

What I know about Corey at the end of this session is that she's interested and eager to write and read her name. I'll use this enthusiasm to build interest in other writing activities. She feels successful with our name work together, and she leaves the session beaming with a feeling of accomplishment.

Attaching guideposts or minimal levels of expectation to phase accomplishments is extremely powerful in helping us make decisions regarding the need for instruction or intervention. A child functioning at Corey's Phase 0 level when she enters kindergarten may already be behind thousands of children who enter kindergarten knowing some letters and knowing how to write their own name. Most of the 1.5 million American children who enter kindergarten with no letter knowledge (West, Denton, & Germino-Hausken, 2000, pp. 22–24) aren't in some developmental lag; their lack of knowledge is due to lack of exposure to print and few book experiences in the home. They haven't been taught how to write their name by their parents or in a preschool setting. Teaching the child to write his or her name is the entry point to early intervention. It comes before letters, sounds, phonological awareness or other parts of literacy because if a child says, "I can write my name" or "I can read my name," she is acknowledging that she is already a reader and a writer. She's using the system and she is already using letters (though not alphabetically). For many children, name writing and name reading are the first giant steps to literacy. The whole *system* of writing one's name can be accomplished as the parts start falling into place.

CHAPTER 2

Phase 1: Operations With Letters but Without Sounds

Phase 1

Key Operations

The child:

- Writes with letters but without letter/sound knowledge
- Uses arbitrary cues for word reading
- Invents spelling with random letters

Critical Aspect

- Nonalphabetic operations with letters

A Phase 1 Vignette: A Grocery List and McDonald's

Let's contrast Phase 0, Corey, with a child who's functioning in Phase 1. Often name writing happens at about the same time as Phase 1 reading of environmental print. The hypothetical child, who happens to be writing her name and showing interest in print, sees the giant McDonald's sign and exclaims, "That says 'McDonald's'!" For the observer, this is a moment of epiphany—this 4-year-old can read! Often the parent that revels in the moment doesn't realize that as wonderful as the event is, the child's not reading as adults read. In fact, she's in Phase 1 and relying on nonalphabetic symbolic cues—in this instance, the golden arches. Phase 1 readers see letters and use them, but their use is not alphabetical. Their letter use excludes matches to sounds. It's fun for Phase 1 children to get in the flow of reading and writing and to use the symbols and letters even though they aren't using them alphabetically. At this phase they don't know how letters represent sounds.

Five-year-old Dan is a Phase 1 writer. He's on the way to the grocery store with his mom and he makes the grocery list presented in Figure 2.2.

His writing of *7Up* is comparable to the Phase 1 reading of *McDonald's*. It's environmental print that he has memorized logographically, and while he may know some numbers and know that 7 represents the number seven, as a Phase 1 reader he doesn't know that *u* stands for /ŭ/ or that *p* stands for /p/. He is two phases away from making analogies that would enable him to analogize and read *cup* or *pup* from *up*. That's coming later. Nevertheless, Dan's literacy is qualitatively different from

7Up, milk, Raisin Bran, doughnuts

FIGURE 2.2 Dan's Grocery List

and much more advanced than Corey's in the Phase 0 sample in Chapter 1. The chart below shows what Dan and his counterparts who read the word *McDonald's* logographically might be expected to do at Phase 1.

Systemic Goals

- Continuing to build interest and confidence in reading
- Continuing to fulfill the child's urge to write
- Engaging the child in the reading and writing *system* by modeling reading and writing and by interacting with the child in reading and writing
- Attending to the parts of reading and writing by directing the child's attention and focusing on particular parts that are important for Phase 1
- Developing awareness of phonology appropriate for Phase 1
- Initiating phase-appropriate language-specific knowledge
  - : Sounds
  - : Letters
  - : Book concepts

Expectations for a Phase 1 Writer

- Knows that writing is meaningful
- Uses letters to represent a message
- May need to be shown how to hold the pencil or pen
- May need to be shown how to position the paper
- May need to be shown how to orient print on the page
- Can name some letters
- Can form some letters
- Exhibits minimal to substantive alphabet knowledge
- Can invent spellings with random letters
- May show a preference for uppercase letters
- May intersperse uppercase and lowercase letters indiscriminately
- May use numerals in invented spelling

- May use unidentifiable characters or incorrect spelling sequences such as double letters to begin a word
- Can write one's own name and a few words
- Illustrates stories from his or her imagination or experience and writes about them in words or phrases, using random letters as shown in Figure 2.3.

FIGURE 2.3

Tweety

Albert's Phase 1 writing: 4 years old

a flock of butterflies

Leslie's Phase 1 writing: 3 years old

Welcome Home

Paul's Phase 1 writing: 4 years old

- Begins to memorize a few Level A easy readers
- Reads back adult underwriting in examples such as those presented in Figure 2.3 on previous page
- Enjoys books
- Develops more sophisticated book-handling concepts

Practical Applications for Phase 1

: Book orientation

: Page-turning

: Directionality

    : Begins to develop a lexicon of sight words stored in memory

    : Does not process letter-sounds systematically

    : Shows signs of matching logos and words

    : Pays attention to nonalphabetic information (Gentry, 2006)

Practical Applications and Explicit Goals for Phase 1

: Memorizing and rereading words and phrases

: Learning to read a few words and phrases from memory

: Storing a few sight words in memory

: Reading back adult underwriting of words and phrases

Expectations for Sound Knowledge at Phase 1

- Phonological awareness such as syllable awareness or recognition of rhyming words is possible
- Phonemic awareness is unlikely or just beginning, with recognition of a few beginning sounds

Practical Applications

: Clapping syllables

: Shouting out or otherwise identifying rhyming words

: Starting to isolate beginning sounds in target words

: Recognizing beginning sounds

: Naming letters

: Matching a few letters to sounds

Key Techniques for Moving Children From Phase 1 to Phase 2

Key techniques for Phase 1 include participation in writing workshop, scaffolded writing, private speech, use of invented spelling, adult underwriting, hand spelling, modeling sound awareness by elongating and accentuating sounds in words, memorizing easy texts, voice-finger pointing, modeling the voice-to-print match, teaching concept of word, and using word walls and other activities to help children begin to build a lexicon of sight words stored in memory.

Scaffolded writing, private speech, and adult underwriting are particularly powerful techniques for Phase 1, and the kindergarten writing workshop offers daily opportunities for teaching and learning from their use.

Suppose we are in a group setting, using a picture and poem chart for "A House Is a House for Me" by Mary Ann Hoberman (Hoberman, 1978; Gentry 2007b). Here's a quick peek at how the teacher might be accommodating instruction to Dan, in Phase 1:

The teacher, using Don Holdaway's technique of reading the chart, reads the poem, modeling the reading as she uses a pointer to point to the words. She eventually moves to reading the poem interactively, engaging the children and employing lots and lots of repetition over time (Holdaway, 1979). As she's reading the following lines, she points to the words, assisting the children in making the voice-to-print match, a strategy designed to help Dan consolidate the concept of word.

A House Is a House for Me

A hill is a house
for an ant, an ant.
A hive is a house
for a bee.
A hole is a house
for a mole
or a mouse,
And a house is a house for me!

As part of the group work with this poem over several days or weeks, the teacher might introduce a hand-spelling activity to help Phase 1 students like Dan pay attention to the beginning /h/ sound, which is prominently featured in this poem. Generally, I encourage teachers to introduce hand spelling, pictured in Figure 2.4, with words that are easier to discriminate, such as *rat*, *cat*, *fat*, and *pat*, featuring the thumb up with the /r/, /k/, /f/, and /p/, respectively. Once students get the hang of hand spelling, they can use the technique to focus attention and hear the beginning /h/ sound in the *h* words featured in the poem: *house*, *hill*, *hive*, and *hole*.

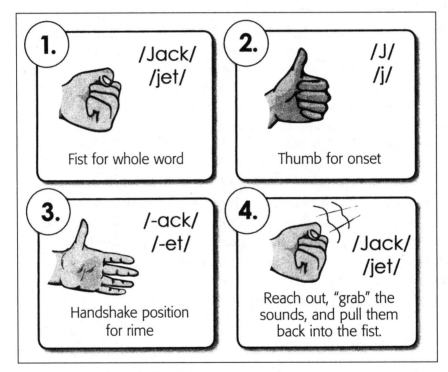

FIGURE 2.4   Hand Spelling Symbols

This group activity of reading from the poem chart using hand spelling is an example of how the teacher might do multilevel instruction in a mixed-ability classroom. Including this activity helps those Phase 1 students like Dan focus attention on beginning sounds such as /h/ in words like *house*. Ultimately, by focusing attention and learning more and more letters and sounds, children at Phase 1 move to the next phase level, Phase 2, where they are able to get beginning letter-sound associations as well as ending and other prominent sounds independently, and operate with partial phonemic awareness.

Word walls may be started with Phase 1 students at the beginning of kindergarten to help them begin to build a lexicon of sight words stored in memory. Organized by the alphabet chart, the kindergarten word wall differs from the more familiar first-grade word wall (Cunningham, 1995; Cunningham & Allington, 1994) in that two rather than five high-frequency words for reading and writing are practiced each week. Multimodal materialization techniques such as clapping and chanting the spellings then writing the word—"*Cat*, *c* (clap), *a* (clap), *t* (clap), *cat*"—repeatedly practiced for about five or ten minutes daily help the child commit these new words to memory. The word wall and child's repertoire of words stored in memory and recognized automatically grow throughout the year. Master kindergarten teacher Isabell Cardonick starts her kindergarten word wall by posting only one word for any particular letter. She includes words such as *and*, *come*, *go*, *I*, *my*, *see*, *rain*, *want*, and *you*. "It teaches the children how to find the word by listening for the first sound, identifying the corresponding beginning letter, and finding that letter on the wall," Cardonick explains. "When a new word is added and there are already one or more words under that letter, I model how to differentiate between the words: 'Hmmm, now we have three words under the letter *c*. If I write the wrong word, then my story might not make sense. My new word-wall word is *could*. *[She exaggerates the /d/ at the end.]* I hear a /d/ at the end. That sound is made with a *d*. So it must be *could* (and not *come* or *can*)'" (Gentry 2006, pp. 102–103). This is a powerful example of nudging children to move them from Phase 1 to Phase 2.

CHAPTER 3

Phase 2: Operations With Partial Phonemic Awareness

Phase 2

Key Operations

The child:

- Writes using partial letter/sound matches
- Cues on beginning letters making partial letter/sound matches for word reading
- Invents abbreviated spellings with partial letter/sound matches

Critical Aspect

- Partial phonemic awareness

A Phase 2 Vignette: The Glorious Entrée to Code Breaking

Figure 3.2 shows Leslie's picture and writing and you can read it.

FIGURE 3.2 Leslie's Phase 2 writing: 6 years old

Had I shown the picture by itself, you probably would not have known what it was. The letter-to-print match, as in Leslie's sample, enables the child to convey meaning at Phase 2, though the match is not complete. It may be restricted to beginning letter/sound matches or, as in the case of HMT DPD for *Humpty Dumpty*, it may be a partial match including ending and other prominent sounds, but in any case, it's the first indication that the child is using the code alphabetically. Phase 2 is another giant step toward literacy. The list below gives us a snapshot of literacy expectations and accomplishments for Phase 2 readers and writers.

Systemic Goals

- Continuing to build interest and confidence in reading
- Increasing volume in writing

- Engaging the child in the reading and writing system with continued modeling of reading and writing, along with continued teacher-child interaction with increasingly sophisticated reading and writing
- Attending to the parts of reading and writing by directing the child's attention and focusing on particular parts that are important for Phase 2, with particular emphasis on expanding knowledge of letter/sound correspondences
- Expanding phonemic awareness
- Continuing to develop phase-appropriate, language-specific knowledge
  - : Sounds
  - : Letters
  - : Book concepts

Expectations for a Phase 2 Writer

- Knows that writing is meaningful
- Uses letters in abbreviated spellings to represent a message
- Generally moves along a *quantitative* continuum for the volume of writing, which generally begins with one-word stories in Phase 1 but often expands rapidly in Phase 2

(*Note: The samples below are not fill-in-the-blank forms. Rather they are intended to model representative phase-appropriate word stories, phrase stories, sentence stories, and multisentence stories, ultimately moving to stories written in several parts.*)

First Samples: One-Word Stories and Labels

Tweety

FIGURE 3.3

Followed by: Phrase Story Frames

Examples include "My _____" stories, "I like _____" stories, and many others, growing into more elaborate and descriptive phrases, such as "My dad's motorboat," and sentences, such as "I like pizza and ice cream."

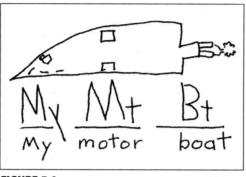

FIGURE 3.4

Followed by: Sentence Story Frames

I like _____ and _____.
A _____ ran over the _____.

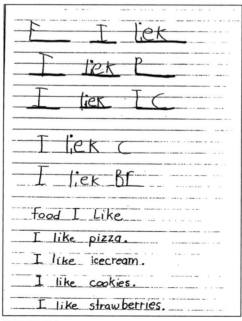

FIGURE 3.5

Followed by: Line Story Frames

Line stories start at three lines and grow to about six lines. An example:

> *My dog is mad.*
> *But I still like her.*
> *We play together.*

Followed by: Elaborate Story Frames

Elaborate story frames may extend from many lines to several pages. Often they are developed in chunks or sections such as these:

BEGINNING	MIDDLE	ENDING

FIRST	THEN	NEXT	LAST

DAY 1	DAY 2	DAY 3	DAY 4	END OF VACATION

Elaborate stories cover an infinite range of topics, including whatever children are interested in and thinking about, and may appear in varying length and formats. Here are two simple examples:

Halloween

I like Halloween
because it is fun!
I went trick or treating.
I dressed as Spiderman.
I went to six houses.

The Runaway Car

My mom was taking too long
so I went to the front seat.

*I didn't mean to but I turned
on the car. My mom ran and ran.
She caught up to the car. I opened
The door. She got in. I was in trouble!
She was mad!*

(Phase 3 and Phase 4 writers often use elaborate story frames like those illustrated above.)

Expectations for a Phase 2 writer, continued:

- Increases ability to match letters to sounds

- Moves toward mastery in naming letters

- Moves toward mastery in forming letters

- Can invent spellings in partial alphabetic representations

- Increases knowledge of letters, graphemes, phonemes, graphophonemic associations, phonological/phonemic awareness, phonological recoding, spelling patterns, and lexicon of sight words already stored in memory

- May intersperse uppercase and lowercase letters indiscriminately but less frequently than at previous phases

- Expands orthographic knowledge such as recognition that it is rarely correct to double letters at the beginnings of words (Wright & Ehri, 2007)

FIGURE 3.6

Humpty Dumpty

In my classroom
Books
Pictures
Friends

FIGURE 3.6 *(CONTINUED)*

Statue of Liberty

- Illustrates stories from his or her imagination or experience and writes about them in words or phrases using partial phonemic awareness, as shown in Figure 3.6

Expectations for a Phase 2 Reader

- Memorizes Level A through Level C readers

- Reads back adult underwriting in examples such as those presented in Figure 3.6

- Continues to enjoy books and receives exposure to a broader range of language through read-alouds

- Stores a lexicon of thirty or more sight words in memory
  (*Note: the particular words a child might have stored in memory at Phase 2 depend on which words he or she has been exposed to. Sight word knowledge at this level may be very difficult to measure reliably and validly on timed tests or sight word recognition tests because of a ceiling effect in the child's repertoire.*)
  Children at Phase 2 may keep a word box or ring clip with sight words for collecting "Words I Can Read."

- Cues on partial alphabetic information (Ehri, 1997; Gentry, 2006)

Practical Applications and Explicit Goals for Phase 2

: Expanding the repertoire of easy-to-read books working from individual collections in book bags or browsing boxes

: Memorizing and rereading words, phrases, and books expanding the repertoire to reading several lines of text or more elaborate stories

: Learning to read more words and phrases from memory

: Storing more sight words in memory

: Reading back adult underwriting of words and phrases

: Reading up to thirty or more word wall words over time

Expectations for Sound Knowledge at Phase 2

- Displays evidence of partial phonemic awareness
- Increases knowledge of letter/sound correspondence
- Demonstrates phonological awareness such as syllable awareness or recognition of rhyming words

Practical Application and Explicit Goals for Phase 2

: Clapping out syllables in words

: Shouting out or otherwise designating rhyming words in poems and nursery rhymes

: Isolating beginning sounds in target words

: Responding well to techniques such as hand spelling for identifying beginning sounds in target words

: Progressing to more difficult phonological awareness tasks

Note: Yopp and Yopp (2000) suggest the progression from easiest to hardest phonemic awareness tasks often moves along the following continuum from less to more sophistication:

Matching: "Which words begin with the same sound?"

Sound Isolation: "What sound do you hear at the beginning of the word *Jack?*"

Sound Substitution: "What word would you have if you change the /j/ in *Jack* to /b/?"

Blending: "What word would you have if you put these sounds together: /j/ plus /ack/?"

Sound Segmentation: "Tell me the sounds you hear in *Jack*."

Sound Deletion: "Say *Jack* without the /j/." "Say Jack without the /k/ at the end."

Move from practice with onsets and rimes and hand spelling (/j/ + /ack/ = *Jack*), a Phase 2 activity, to blending phonemes or finger spelling, which is a Phase 3 activity (/j/-/a/-/k/ = *Jack*).

Leslie is in a small guided reading group with other Phase 2 readers, and they are working this week with "Jack Be Nimble." They work with the rhyme from a chart, reading it in unison as Leslie, who volunteers to lead the group in a choral reading, uses a pointer to point to the words. They have done this procedure repeatedly, and now all six of the children can read the poem from memory. They can also read the poem to their peers and to parents from their own eight-page "keep books" that the children have made and illustrated at school, and that they use for extra practice and additional rereading and repetition.

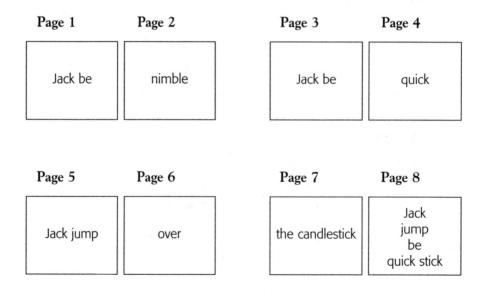

Page 1 — Jack be

Page 2 — nimble

Page 3 — Jack be

Page 4 — quick

Page 5 — Jack jump

Page 6 — over

Page 7 — the candlestick

Page 8 — Jack jump be quick stick

Working with picture cards illustrating *jar, jump, Jack, jeep, jet, bed, bus, bat,* and *bee* (Gentry & Craddock, 2005), the teacher leads the Phase 2 reading group in a word sort focusing on the /j/ and the /b/ sounds, using a hand spelling technique:

Teacher: What word does this picture represent?

Students: *Jack.*

Teacher: Let's hand-spell it together. What's the first sound that you hear in *Jack*? Listen as I say it. /j/, /ack/, *Jack*. Now you try it. Remember, hold up your thumb as you say the first sound.

Students: [*Sticking up their thumbs*] /j/.

Teacher: Now say the rest of it as you make the handshake position.

Students: [*Forming the handshake position*] /ack/.

Teacher: Now reach out and grab those sounds and say the whole word!

Students: *Jack!*

The group proceeds to use the hand-spelling technique to focus attention on beginning sounds of other words selected randomly from the picture card stack: *jet, bat, jeep, bus, bat,* and so forth.

Teacher: That was great. Now get a partner, and we'll do a word sort. I'll give each buddy team a stack of the cards. Find the *Jack* card and put that one at the top. Find the *bed* card and put that one next to the *Jack* card. You will be making two columns. The first will be a column of words that begin like *Jack*. The next will be a column of words that begin like *bed*. What sound will the words that begin like *Jack* begin with?

Students: /j/.

Teacher: What sound will the words that begin like *bed* begin with?

Students: /b/.

The students sort their picture cards into the two categories, discussing and practicing the beginning sounds as they work together.

Teacher: You did a nice job. You have all completed your sorts. I see the two columns—words like *Jack* and words like *bed*. Now, turn the *Jack* card over and you will see the same picture of Jack with the word *Jack* written underneath. What letter does *Jack* start with?

Students: *J !*

Teacher: That's right. *J* makes the /j/ sound. Now do the same thing with *bed*. What letter does *bed* start with?

Students: *B!*

Teachers: Yes, and *b* makes the /b/ sound. Now turn over all the words in each column. See if all the words in your *Jack* column start with *J*. See if all the words in your *bed* column start with *B*. Can you point to each word in each column and read them to your buddy?

Reading the sight words is the last step of this exemplary Phase 2 teacher-led sort, which has focused on beginning sounds. It introduces whole words and challenges the Phase 2 reader to pay attention to all letters—a move to Phase 3.

Key Techniques for Moving Children From Phase 2 to Phase 3

As in Phase 2, key techniques for Phase 3 include participation in writing workshop, scaffolded writing, private speech (for some children at the beginning of Phase 3), use of invented spelling, adult underwriting, hand spelling, modeling sound awareness by elongating and accentuating sounds in words, voice-finger pointing, modeling the voice-to-print match, teaching the concept of word-for-word sequences such as "once upon a time" (which is sometimes spelled as one word: ONSAPNATIM), and using word walls and other activities to help children continue to build a lexicon of sight words stored in memory. The objective is to increase the child's knowledge about various parts or features of literacy and to increase the level of sophistication of what she can do both qualitatively and quantitatively. The move from Phase 2 to Phase 3 is signified by growing independence in both reading and writing. As the child's sophistication grows, she will discontinue the use of private speech and may no longer need scaffolded writing or even adult underwriting. Both writing workshop and guided reading offer daily opportunities for the child to grow as a reader and a writer.

Scaffolded Writing

Let's imagine how the teacher might nudge a Phase 2 writer like Leslie to write a story like "Humpty Dumpty" using scaffolded writing and private speech. The teacher might begin with a discussion of a drawing such as the one in Figure 3.7. After viewing the drawing together, the teacher would ask Leslie to talk about it.

1. Drawing

2. "Tell me about your picture."

3. Lines in scaffold

4. Private speech

5. Child's writing

6. Adult underwriting

7. Reading and rereading adult underwriting

FIGURE 3.7 Activity sequences

Teacher: Tell me about your picture.

Leslie: It's Humpty Dumpty!

Teacher: Let's write "Humpty Dumpty" above your picture! We'll write it on these lines that I make with this yellow marker. [*The teacher makes two lines with a yellow highlighter—one for "Humpty" and one for "Dumpty." If one word happens to be considerably longer than the other, she would make a short line and a longer one. As the teacher scaffolds the writing with a yellow marker, she says the words that Leslie will write on each of the lines:* Humpty *and* Dumpty.]

Private Speech

Teacher: Now, Leslie, read what goes on each line as I point to it. [*The teacher points to the lines consecutively.*]

Leslie: Humpty Dumpty.

Teacher:	That's great. Read what goes on the lines again. What goes on this first line?
Leslie:	Humpty.
Teacher:	What comes next?
Leslie:	Dumpty.
Teacher:	Now read the whole thing. [*Pointing to the two lines*]
Leslie:	Humpty Dumpty!

The repetition of the words to go on the lines is a kind of rehearsal or planning stage for writing called "private speech." It not only helps the child plan and frame the "story" to be written but also creates independence in the writer. Using scaffolded writing and private speech together allows the teacher to leave this mini-conference having shown Leslie exactly how to proceed on her own. Private speech is when the writer repeats words or a phase to be written to give himself or herself auditory directions to support the mental action of writing these same words on the page (Bodrova and Leong, 1998).

Adult Underwriting

Adult underwriting is the most powerful technique for connecting writing and reading directly and for allowing inventive spellers at beginning phase levels to have exposure to a conventional English version of the story they write from their imagination. With adult underwriting, beginning readers read and reread an adult version of whatever they wrote. This version is easier to read and provides more cues than the version containing their own invented spellings. Here the teacher invites Leslie to read the adult underwriting of her message, which the teacher refers to as "kid writing."

Teacher:	Wow, Leslie. That's great kid writing. At the bottom of the page [*in the same word and line order*], I'll show you what "Humpty Dumpty" looks like in adult writing. Here it is: "Humpty Dumpty." Read the kid writing. [*Teacher points to Leslie's writing*]
Leslie:	Humpty Dumpty.
Teacher:	Now read the adult underwriting.
Leslie:	Humpty Dumpty.

Teacher: Leslie. You can read adult writing! And look how many letters you have that are in the adult writing. I want you to practice reading this adult writing over and over. Do you think you can read it for me tomorrow? Do you think you can practice it so that you can read it to me if we come back to this page next week?

Leslie: I can do that!

Now contrast what Leslie can do at Phase 2 with what Sarah can do in Phase 3.

CHAPTER 4

Phase 3: Operations With Full Phonemic Awareness

Phase 3

Key Operations

The child:

- Writes using complete letter/sound matches
- Attends to full letter/sound matches for word reading
- Invents spellings with one letter for each sound in a word

Critical Aspect

- Full phonemic awareness; spelling patterns are not represented in chunks

Breakthrough in Beginning Reading and Writing

A Phase 3 Vignette: Reading and Writing Take Off

Contrast Leslie, in Phase 2, who is writing HMP DPD for *Humpty Dumpty* and reading "Jack Be Nimble" from memory, with Sarah, in Phase 3, who is just starting first grade. Sarah can read a fairly long story about Max the Cat in partially decodable text from her beginning first-grade-level basal with confidence and fluency, apparently having practiced it over and over. By calling out a few words in a simple spelling check and by glancing at spelling in Sarah's writing, I notice that she has already mastered many short-vowel patterns—*nap, mat, hug,* and *sad,* which is advanced for Phase 3, since these patterns generally aren't spelled correctly until the end of Phase 3 and aren't consistently spelled correctly until Phase 4. At the same time, it's clear that Sarah still uses a few Phase 3 short-vowel spellings such as WIT for *went* with *I* for the short *e* and the predictable omission of the *n* for the preconsonantal nasal. She also spells *let* as LIT, a typical Phase 3 spelling when children often use A for short *e,* E for short *i,* I for short *o,* and O for short *u,* due to the sound of the letter name and its closeness in place of articulation to the contrasting short vowel sound. Sarah's teacher says Sarah has increased the volume and repertoire of what she can read and that she's one of the better readers in her class. Sarah feels like a reader and she loves to read and to write.

When I meet her in September of her first-grade year, at Phase 3, Sarah is already a master writer of three- and four-line stories. She shows me some of her favorites:

Story	Spelling Analysis
My dog is mad *or she is sad* *But I STEL like her* *We play TOGETTR*	STEL is Phase 3, a letter for each sound. TOGETTR is Phase 3 with its TR spelling of the *r*-controlled vowel.
I have a ELEFIT *He is big*	ELEFIT is Phase 3 due to the omission of the preconsonantal *n.*
And STOG	STOG is Phase 2 because the /r/ is omitted, but with the characteristic Phase 3 omission of the preconsonantal nasal *n.*

Story	Spelling Analysis (continued)
I see a pig ROLIND in the mud.	ROLIND, Phase 3, has a letter for each sound.
I see a cow moo, moo, moo. I see a hen TO.	This sample demonstrates Sarah's early strong knowledge of short vowels and digraph spelling for Phase 3.

Note: For some invented spelling, it's hard to determine whether the spelling is Phase 3 or Phase 4 just by seeing the final product. There are two examples of this phenomenon in the last sample above. ROLIND for rolling (Sarah pronounced the word with a /d/ at the end) and TO for too may either be a Phase 3 letter-for-each-sound spelling or Phase 4 chunking spelling. The best way to tell is to watch the child's strategy for forming the spelling; if it is slow and analytical, with the child putting down a letter for each sound much like finger spelling, it's Phase 3. (This is the strategy that Sarah used.) If the child is analogizing, it's Phase 4.

In a demonstration in front of 45 teachers, Sarah and I talked about her reading and writing, and she shared her stories and read "Max the Cat" out loud from the basal. I suggested that we might have fun writing a story together in front of the teachers. She agreed. We started by *planning* the story—really just having a freewheeling conversation until I found a topic we might dig into. We settled on a chat about her dog, Chiquita, and Sarah joyfully told us all about her pet, answering my questions about its name, where she got it, what it eats, and so forth.

Here's how it went:

Gentry: Can you tell us one funny story about Chiquita? Can you think of a moment in time when something happened that made you laugh?

Sarah relays a funny story that results in a story called "Chiquita's Bath." I give her the following first-then-next-last story framework, and as we begin to write the story in front of the teachers, I "talk" Sarah through each frame.

FIRST	THEN	NEXT	LAST

Gentry:　Okay, Sarah, how shall we start the story? Tell me something you said that leads us into this story.

Sarah thinks about it and starts to write the part of the story ending with "One day my mom decided to give Chiquita a bath."

Gentry:　Then what happened?

Sarah writes the next two lines.

Gentry:　What happened next?

Sarah writes, "I got the soap." To nudge her to put in some detail, I ask how she thought Chiquita felt, and Sarah writes the next three lines. We now have a ten-line story, and I can see that Sarah is getting a little tired. We need to finish it, though, and go back and put in a title, so I nudge a little more because this is happening in front of an audience, and I will not be available tomorrow to help finish the story. (I'm reminded to point out to the teachers that what Sarah accomplishes in this demonstration would generally take more time, typically happening over several sessions in a writing workshop.) I'm hoping Sarah will include the funny part of the story she relayed in our conversation, when the wet dog jumped into her bed.

Gentry:　Let's end with the funny part!

Sarah completes her story.

Here's a corrected version of Sarah's story. Our Phase 3, three-line writer is moving into more elaborate story writing!

Chiquita's Bath

Chiquita likes to
SLIPS [sleep] WETH [with] me. One day
my mom DESIDET [decided] to
give Chiquita a

bath. I HOD [held] Chiquita.

Mom had to get a TAVEOL [towel].

I got the SOP [soap].

She DUSET [doesn't] like

for me to TECK [take]

her a bath. I LIT [let]

her go and

she WIT [went] UNTR [under] the CUVRS [covers].

Ten of the twelve invented spellings in the story are Phase 3, including WETH for *with*, DESIDET for *decided*, SOP for *soap*, WIT for *went*, UNTR for *under*, and CUVRS for *covers*—an excellent example of Phase 3 writing. There were twenty-three correctly spelled words in the story, including many words that might have been learned from word-wall work such as *me, day, my, mom, a, I, had, to, get, got, the, she, like, for her,* and *and,* and *go.* This is another striking contrast between Phase 3 Sarah and Phase 2 Leslie: Sarah is demonstrating that she is getting a large repertoire of sight words and correctly spelled words in her memory and can recognize when to use them.

In guided reading over the next few weeks or months, if Sarah's development is typical of Phase 3, she will progress from Level C to Level H or above. There will be lots of focus on word families to quickly build her store of sight words. She will continue with word-wall work. It's likely during this period that Sarah will begin to make analogies to known words, a strategy that is not common at Phase 2 but generally kicks in at Phase 3. So if Sarah knows *nap, mat, hug,* and *sad,* she may begin analogizing to figure out new words that she encounters in print for the first time, figuring out that *trap* is analogous to *nap, sat* to *mat, tug* to *hug, dad* to *sad,* and so on.

Not only do many Phase 3 readers like Sarah rapidly build their repertoire of stories at Levels C and higher, but they *enjoy* reading more—especially repeated readings of their favorite stories—and the increase in volume adds to their fluency and word-specific knowledge.

Sarah enjoys the discussions and book talks surrounding stories read aloud to her, which aid comprehension, sense of story, and her academic vocabulary. While she might not be able to read a story like Robert Munsch's *Alligator Baby* (1997) if she just picked up the book and tried reading it on her own, she can follow the story if it's read aloud in class first. Indeed, she can easily join in reading chosen sections of the text chorally with her classmates as the teacher divides the class into three roles (Mother, Kristen, and the Noise Makers), models the three parts illustrated below, and invites children to participate in the read-aloud of this wonderful piece of children's literature.

Mother: Kristen, would you like to see your new baby brother?

Kristen: Oh, yes.
That's not a people tail.
That's not a people arm.
That's not a people face.
That is *not* my baby brother.

Mother: Now, Kristen, don't be jealous.

Noise Makers: Varooooooooooommmm.
Blam, blam, blam, blam, blam.
Aaaaaahhhhhaaaaa!

Activities such as this are extremely important for helping children at Phase 3 develop fluency, motivation, and interest in reading, and build their vocabularies and comprehension of sophisticated texts.

Here Is a Summary of Phase 3:

Systemic Goals

- Extending interest and confidence in reading
- Continuing to increase volume in writing
- Continuing to engage the child in the reading and writing system
- Attending to the parts of reading and writing by directing the child's attention and focusing on particular parts that are important for Phase 3
- Expanding phonemic awareness

FIGURE 4.2

Key Sound-Symbol Relationships to Assess and Teach

Focus on the following high-frequency sound-symbol relationships first:

a as in *bat*	g as in *goat*	o-e as in *home*
m	l	v
t	o as in *hot*	e as in *bed*
s	h	u-e as in *use*
i as in *hit*	u as in *cup*	p
f	b	w as in *wet*
a-e as in *cake*	n	j
d	k	i-e as in *like*
r	y as in *yoke*	z

Once these are mastered, focus on the following:

ch as in *chip*	ou as in *cloud*	kn as in *knot*
ea as in *meat*	oy as in *boy*	oa as in *boat*
ee as in *need*	ph as in *phone*	oi as in *boil*
er as in *her*	qu as in *quick*	ai as in *maid*
ay as in *day*	sh as in *ship*	ar as in *car*
igh as in *high*	th as in *thank*	au as in *haul*
ew as in *new*	ir as in *girl*	aw as in *paw*

Adapted from *The Literacy Map: Guiding Children to Where They Need to Be* (Gentry, 1998).

This chart is based on Burmeister's research (1975), which identified a set of approximately 45 letter-sound correspondences that have a utility rate high enough to justify instruction.

Practical Applications for Phase 3

Continuation and Extension of Phase 2 Goals

: Note any letters or basic sounds that aren't known.

: Use the chart in Figure 4.2 to identify key sound-symbol associations.

: Continuing to develop phase-appropriate, language-specific knowledge

: Sound-symbol associations in Figure 4.2

: Consonant-Vowel-Consonant (CVC)

Expectations for a Phase 3 Writer

- Knows that writing is meaningful

- Uses a letter for each sound when inventing spellings

- Generally moves along a *quantitative* continuum for the volume of writing, which generally begins with one-word stories in Phase 1, expands rapidly in Phase 2, and moves to more elaborate story frames in Phase 3

- Invents spellings in full alphabetic representations

- Increases knowledge of graphophonemic associations, phonological/phonemic awareness, phonological recoding, spelling patterns, and lexicon of sight words already stored in memory

- Expands orthographic knowledge such as use of analogies

- Illustrates stories from his or her imagination or experience and writes about them in words or phrases using full phonemic awareness, as shown in Figure 4.3

FIGURE 4.3

Kevin's Phase 3 spelling

Meredith's Phase 3 writing: 5 years, 3 months old

FIGURE 4.3 (CONTINUED)

EF U KAN OPN KAZ I WILL GEV U A KN OPENR

If you can open cans I will give you a can opener.

Paul's Phase 3 writing: 5 years, 2 months old

Expectations for a Phase 3 Reader

- Memorizes Level C (and higher) readers
- Reads back adult underwriting in examples such as those presented in Figure 4.3 above, but adult underwriting is phased out toward the end of Phase 3
- Continues to enjoy books and receives exposure to a broader range through read-alouds
- Stores lexicon of up to one hundred sight words in memory
- Cues on full alphabetic information (Ehri, 1997; Gentry, 2006)

Practical Applications and Explicit Goals for Phase 3

- : Expanding the repertoire of easy-to-read books, working from individual collections in book bags or browsing boxes
- : Memorizing and rereading books, expanding the repertoire of more elaborate stories
- : Storing more sight words in memory

Expectations for Sound Knowledge at Phase 3

- Evidence of full phonemic awareness
- Increased knowledge of letter/sound correspondence

Key Techniques for Moving Children from Phase 3 to Phase 4

Writing typically moves to more elaborate forms in Phase 3, allowing children to write fairly sophisticated accounts of what they experience or think about. Thoughts from their imagination often grow in length to two or three pages or more. Extensive use of word families facilitates the Phase 3 child's use of analogies, greatly increasing his or her access to new words. Pattern-recognition work should proceed in many formats, with extensive onset and rime work focusing on the rime pattern—with particular emphasis on basic vowel patterns, especially CVC short vowels in words such as *cap, pet, bit, hop,* and *cut* and eventually CVCe such as *cape, Pete, bite, hope,* and *cute.* Children will begin contrasting and solidifying these patterns in Phase 4, signifying the move to more complex pattern recognition and chunking.

CHAPTER 5

Phase 4:
Operations With Full Code
and Chunking Knowledge

Phase 4

Key Operations

The child:

- Writes operating with chunks of phonics patterns
- Attends to chunking for word reading
- Invents spelling in chunks of letter patterns

Critical Aspect

- Operations occur with knowledge of how the code works; spelling patterns are represented in chunks.

A Phase 4 Vignette: The Reader/Writer Breaks the Code

The best way to assess a reader or a writer is to ask her to show you what she can do and have her tell you about it. "Show me the reading and writing you are doing" is what I always ask once I know that a child is Phase 1 or higher. (If she is Phase 0, I ask her to write her name.) I want to see what she can do with the system of reading and writing. I have her bring in her "browsing box" or book bag as well as her writing folder with the last few months of her productions. If one understands phase theory, one generally can pinpoint a child's level of development in just a few minutes. The writing folder, browsing box and a short interview with the child provide powerful data. I used this interview technique when I met Uma for the first time.

My conversation with Uma began this way:

Gentry: Hi, Uma. Tell me about yourself. What grade are you in, and how old are you?

Uma: I'm in first grade. I'm six.

This is my first clue to Uma's level of functioning. I anticipate that a six-year-old in December of first grade should be Phase 3, or if she is making really good progress, Phase 4.

Gentry: Tell me about the books you are reading. Show me the ones in your book basket.

Uma: This is a book called *Henry and Mudge and the Bedtime Thumps* by Cynthia Rylant.

In this instance, I know that the *Henry and Mudge* books are second-grade level. If Uma can actually read *Henry and Mudge*—she's beyond the typical mid-first-grade level and likely in Phase 4 or above. I ask Uma to start reading at a page that I pick at random, and my hypothesis that she's well above grade level is confirmed. I stop her after about three pages as she glides effortlessly into the words "soon he began to bite his fingernails." Already, I see the big picture of Uma as a reader and perhaps even a writer—this child has broken the code. She reads *Henry and Mudge* as fluently and smoothly as I can. She's well beyond finger pointing and the choppy word-by-word renditions typical of some Phase 3 readers who recite memorized text. Her comprehension is completely intact, which is readily apparent from the level of sophistication with which she responds to my questions and from the detail and erudition with which her retelling comes forth. When Uma reads, her brain likely processes the text just as a skilled adult reader's would—automatically.

As Uma continues to tell me about her reading, she provides additional evidence and confirmation that she is above grade level and well beyond the beginning of Phase 4. Her discussion of her reading is sophisticated. She talks about reading series books and discusses her favorite authors. Her recollection and retelling of books she has recently read includes elaborate recall, detail, synthesis, and analysis. "This is a book you learn to make gifts from," she says as she shows me one book. "This is a Spanish folktale, and this is a chapter book," she says as she shows me others. She makes text-to-text, text-to-self, and other sophisticated connections when we zero in on a page or chapter, and she can do thoughtful critiques or easily launch into an overview that verifies the deep level of thinking that characterizes her reading. "This is a book from a series, and it's about a giant who has a very bad cold and they give him something to make him better—it's medicine," she tells me, perfectly summarizing one of her choices. She has become a reader who reads for her own purposes with fluency and comprehension. Academic and advanced vocabulary sparkle throughout her discussion, reflecting the ideas and vocabulary in the literature she is describing.

Drawing from reading and writing reciprocity and phase theory, I raise my expectations for Uma's writing now that I can see what she can do as a reader. As I glance at her writing, what's immediately apparent in her Phase 4 samples is that she "gets" how the code works. She operates with a chunking system, spelling with acceptable phonics patterns and with a high level of word-specific knowledge, employing many words already stored in her memory. When she writes her ideas down, meaning drives the system; she has passed beyond the slow and analytical phases where she had to think a lot about how to handle the sounds in most words. Now many spellings come to her automatically—she has activated Area C of the brain—and when she does need an unknown word, she analogizes using the chunks of letter combinations that she knows. If she knows that *air* is A-I-R, for example, she may spell *where* as WH-AIR.

Though Uma's writing and spelling match my expectations, I might just as well have begun my assessment with her writing or spelling, because reading, writing, and spelling all tie into one another systemically. In the beginning phases, reading, writing and spelling work in concert. When I ask Uma to spell some words on the Monster Test (Gentry, 2007a), she spells all but one of the first five correctly, signaling that she is functioning at the end-of-second-grade or third-grade level as a speller. Next I look at the spellings in Uma's writing samples and immediately see a high level of sophistication both in the number of words spelled correctly and, perhaps more important, in the quality of her inventions— all clearly Phase 4 renditions. Every invented spelling is spelled in chunks of acceptable phonics patterns and letter combinations.

There's BOTUM for *bottom*, SPESHIL for *special*, TEMPEL for *temple*, TO for *too*, BEFOR for *before*, COSINS for *cousins*, LEVE for *leave*, GRATE for *great*, BY for *bye*, and TELS for *tells*. Predictably, Uma is dealing with spelling issues that one would see addressed in a good, research-based second- or third-grade spelling curriculum, such as when to change the *y* to *i* and add *-es*, as in STORYS for *stories*, and the complexities of *s* and *es*, as in her use of LIVSE for *lives*. She's also dealing with the variety of possible vowel digraph patterns, which is a hallmark of late second- and third-grade spelling, as illustrated by GRATE for *great*, LEVE for *leave*, SPESHIL for *special*, and COSINS for *cousins*—words in which the *-ea*, *-ia*, and *-ou* patterns come into play.

Uma's spelling accuracy in writing—almost 80 percent of all words are spelled correctly in the samples I inspected, which included 65 different words—match my expectations for a third-grade-level speller and is better than the typical one-third of running words misspelled that one often sees in spelling at the beginning second-grade-level spelling. (Gentry, 2005)

Uma is no longer a "tadpole" developing in phases. She has matured into an adultlike reader, writer, and speller. She has topped out at Phase 4 and moved beyond. Her basic literacy skills seem automatic: as with riding a bike, now that she has learned the skills, she's not likely to falter. With access, motivation, and interest, she will move to higher levels of reading and diversity in content. Not only is she a skilled and proficient reader, she writes with relative ease, and the content is driving the process. She has enough spelling and word-specific knowledge that many words come automatically, leaving her free to apply the major brain power to delivering her message rather than worrying about spelling. She's soaring!

Let's see what expectations and goals match Phase 4.

Systemic Goals

- Extending interest and confidence in reading
- Continuing to increase volume of writing in new and various genres
- Moving toward complete reading independence

Practical Applications for Phase 4

Continuation and Extension of Phase 3 Goals

: Explicit spelling instruction moving to grade-level two or higher
spelling curriculum

: Word sorting to develop chunking knowledge and extend ability
to analogize

: Chunking knowledge should grow exponentially at Phase 4. Work
includes identifying high-frequency patterns and contrasts such as the
chunking patterns in Figure 5.2.

FIGURE 5.2

Consonant-Vowel-Consonant and
Consonant-Vowel-Consonant-Vowel Matched Pairs

bit, bite	cub, cube	cut, cute
can, cane	cap, cape	cod, code
con, cone	Dan, Dane	dim, dime
fad, fade	fat, fate	fin, fine
fir, fire	hat, hate	hid, hide
hop, hope	kit, kite	Jan, Jane
man, mane	mad, made	mat, mate
not, note	pal, pale	pan, pane
pin, pine	rat, rate	rod, rode
rip, ripe	rob, robe	sit, site
Sam, same	Sid, side	Tim, time
tam, tame	tap, tape	van, vane
Tom, tome	tub, tube	win, wine

(Shaywitz, 2003, p. 214)

Word Sorting

Word sorting is a core instruction strategy for developing chunking and word-specific knowledge in Phase 4 and beyond. It is a research-based way to develop automatic control of spelling patterns based on the fact that the brain learns to do things automatically by firing neurons over and over. Sorting words in particular patterns in teacher-led sorts, individual sorts, buddy sorts, speed sorts, and the like is hugely beneficial, allowing repetition to lead to automaticity with important patterns. As children sort word cards into columns based on spelling patterns, they engage in conceptual, hands-on, collaborative, student-friendly, theoretically sound, and empirically supported spelling instruction (Bear, Invernizzi, Templeton, & Johnston, 2000; Brown & Morris 2005; Gentry, 2004; Zutell, 1992, 1999). This brain-based sorting strategy helps Phase 3 and 4 pupils develop word-specific knowledge for both writing and reading (Gentry, 2006).

Once Phase 3 pupils automatically recognize CVC patterns by sorting words such as *cap*, *hat*, *pet*, *hen*, *hop*, and *cut* or *put*, they move to a higher level, using sorting tasks to spell contrasting patterns such as *cap* and *cape*, *hop* and *hope*, and *cut* and *cute*. As they move to even higher levels, they move to automatic recognition and production of even more sophisticated variations on the same pattern as well as newly introduced patterns. Eventually students move from recognition and production of *hop* and *hope* to patterns of regularity such as *hopping* and *hoping* or *hopped* and *hoped*. By word sorting in an appropriate curriculum of word study for spelling, they establish and stabilize their word knowledge as it grows by degrees and in sophistication (Gentry, 2007b).

Word sort options include the following:

Teacher-Led Sorts

Teacher-led sorts are an opportunity for the teacher to teach the pattern, to show how the pattern might contrast with another pattern, and to model how the sort is done. Once the teacher teaches a pattern, students might share in sorting the words under the direction of the teacher.

Individual Sorts

Students sort independently for individual practice. Phase 4 students might keep a notebook of patterns studied and write each sort in column formation.

Writing the sort in column formation not only aids in the learning of the pattern but also serves as a record of which word sorts or chunking patterns a student has studied.

Buddy Sorts

Buddy sorts take advantage of the social context of learning and allow for repetition and practice under highly motivational circumstances. Buddy sorts greatly increase the number of times students engage with the unit pattern and lead to automaticity.

Speed Sorts

Speed sorting leads to automatic recognition and production of the spelling patterns being studied. Students may speed-sort individually, sorting a stack of word cards representing the target patterns as fast as they can, or they may compete against their classmates to see who can complete a sort the fastest and with the greatest number of words sorted correctly (Gentry, 2007b). Focus on a variety of double-vowel patterns once a child enters Phase 4, such as *ea*, *ee*, *ay*, *oa*, *oi*, *ai*, and *au*.

Expectations for a Phase 4 Writer

- Can invent spellings in chunks
- Spells correctly more than half of the words in a fairly lengthy piece, independently written
- Continues to increase knowledge of graphophonemic associations, phonological/phonemic awareness, phonological recoding, spelling patterns, and lexicon of sight words already stored in memory
- Continues to expand orthographic knowledge such as use of analogies, adding many new chunking patterns to the repertoire
- Illustrates stories from his or her imagination or experience and writes about them, spelling unknown words in chunks as shown in Figure 5.3

FIGURE 5.3

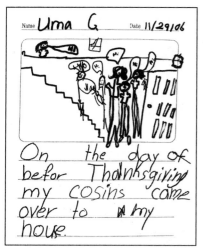

Name **Uma G** Date **11/29/06**

On the day of befor Thanksgiving my cosins come over to my houe.

I was dancing for them and they likd it and I felt proud.

On Thanksging my cosins left I was sad Becase I did not want them to leve.

Uma's Phase 4 writing on Thanksgiving

Name **Uma G** Date **11/27/06**

Ganasha thers move

India is where I come from. I think india is speshel speshil. India even has gods with four arms!

We pray to gods in the tempel they have lots of names.

Mahabora

I Love youDto!
I lov you

I loke india because my grandma livse ther A and she tels grate starys!

Uma's Phase 4 writing on India

Expectations for a Phase 4 Reader

- Most likely moves beyond Level G texts
- Drops need to memorize and exhibits independence
- Continues to enjoy books and receives exposure to a broader range of them, including chapter books
- Stores lexicon of more than a hundred sight words in memory

Practical Applications and Explicit Goals for Phase 4

- : Expands the repertoire of books in individual collections in book bag or browsing box
- : Increases knowledge of letter/sound correspondence
- : Increases knowledge of words correctly spelled from memory

Moving Beyond Phase 4

Phase 4 instruction consists of comprehensive guided reading instruction with an emphasis on encouraging comprehension and fluency, introducing texts in new genres and at higher levels of difficulty, and explicit spelling instruction. The curriculum typically begins at about second-grade level and spirals upward. The reader or writer moves beyond the developmental phase levels into mature reading and writing and into a spelling curriculum that may be designated by grade levels.

An understanding of phase theory will help you see how current practices in reading education in America need to change. Using the five phases of code breaking as a guide, Part II demonstrates how we can be more strategic in teaching and assessment, and how we can implement more effective policy and overhaul teacher preparation for beginning literacy.

Why We Must Become Strategic About Code-Breaking

A strategic approach to helping all beginning readers and writers break the code is long overdue and urgently needed if America is to meet the educational challenges of the twenty-first century. The chapters that follow pave the way for new thinking and appropriate action—to move us forward in the successful teaching of beginning reading and writing, from policy changes to understanding our history to a commitment to keep learning.

In Chapter 6 we learn about teaching within systems of reading and writing reciprocity even as we pay attention to the parts and provide the right instruction at the right time. Chapter 7 celebrates the contributions of Reading Recovery but also challenges Reading Recovery to move forward. Chapter 8 clarifies the clear path of phase theory, and Chapter 9 provides powerful new insights about phonics instruction. Part II ends with a call to action in the twenty-first century.

CHAPTER 6

Two Revolutionary Instructional Shifts for America's Kindergartens and First Grades

P hase theory paves the way for two revolutionary instructional shifts for America's kindergartens and first grades:

1. Teach the whole system including the parts from the very beginning— teach writing *and* reading first.

2. Respond to what the child is doing in each phase with the right instruction at the right time using precise methods and materials to move the child to the next level. Allow beginning writing to drive the reading program.

Get Going With the System— Teach Writing *and* Reading First

Many American kindergartens are junkyards where children rummage around looking for spare parts for the reading machine. We give them this part and that part, and then they are supposed to put the machine together on their own. Because many educators think that phonemic awareness is the driving component that cranks up the reading machine, you will see children sorting words, practicing letters, spending 15 minutes a day on "phonemic awareness," practicing fluency, and doing vocabulary work or comprehension questions with the teacher. None of these are bad experiences, and some have moved us far beyond former decades of woefully inadequate kindergarten curricula that used to suspend literacy instruction until first grade. Yet preparing our kindergartners for the phonemic-awareness and letter-knowledge tests doesn't help them put the system together. Phase theory suggests it's more natural for the system to be driven by writing, with phonemic awareness developing both naturally and with explicit instruction.

In reading, the *system* comes first, and the parts are an outgrowth of using it. It's the same with learning to ride a bike, catch a fish, speak a language, or play a musical instrument. One starts by getting a handle on the meaningful system. Kids get interested in it, pay attention, try it out, notice the patterns, and try to fix their mistakes when they mess up. They use the system over and over and get better at it. Some of the harder parts need more attention. Some of the parts become automatic.

If you go to Ed.gov (http://www.ed.gov/nclb/methods/whatworks/doing.html), the official site for the No Child Left Behind Act, you will learn about various research-based components of reading. I would agree that these are scientifically-based and highly important, but they are very abstract and complex. If you are using scientific evidence to enhance children's reading skills, and you focus exclusively on "the five key areas that scientifically based reading research has identified as essential components of reading instruction—phonemic awareness, phonics, vocabulary, fluency, and reading comprehension" (Ed.gov), are you teaching the system or just its parts?

While I recognize advances resulting from No Child Left Behind, the current centerpiece of America's education agenda, including greater accountability, I now worry about overuse of testing, inadequate assessments, and a stymied, test-driven curriculum that restricts teachers and perhaps blocks efforts to move pedagogy forward. Here's one example: I was recently invited to train the Reading First teacher core of a large Northeastern state. I suggested to the coordinator that there were better things to do in Reading First's mandated 90-minute reading block than have the phonemic-awareness period, the phonics period, the vocabulary period, the fluency period, and the comprehension period, but she wanted the "spare parts" seminar because the law mandated a spare parts curriculum. In a law called Reading First, there was no room for writing. She didn't approve when I suggested that children should joyfully write and read back their own thoughts during the 90-minute *reading* block—even though they were *reading* back what they had written! She didn't understand reading and writing reciprocity or that a teacher could write the correct spellings under a child's scribbles or invented spellings to show him or her the whole system. This coordinator didn't recognize the research base for this type of instruction, and she missed the explicit, systematic, and intensive phonics instruction that grows naturally, sequentially, and without guesswork out of the child's early writing experiences. She didn't realize that writing for reading would complement and enhance the important Reading First goals. She had read *Breaking the Code* (Gentry, 2006), but she'd missed the point of reading/writing reciprocity—that when children read back the adult underwriting of the stories they have written, it's reading! She seemed mystified by the suggestion that the beginning writer is activating the same neurological systems that are activated for reading and that the beginning reading and writing systems "are one and the same, almost" (Ehri, 1997). In her mind, the law required the child to get going with the parts and not with the system. I wonder if that is really the law's intent. In the end, she withdrew my contract.

In his 1973 treatise, *Psycholinguistics and Reading*, Frank Smith got at the heart of beginning reading instruction when he said that children learn to read by reading and that the secret to helping children learn to read was "to make reading easy" (p. 195). In kindergarten reading, this means repeating a nursery rhyme or a little story over and over until the child knows it from memory and gets into the flow of "reading." The first little "books" (easy Level A readers), the child's own stories written down and transcribed by adult underwriting into conventional text, and little poems or nursery rhymes may have three to five words on a page, a concept the child is interested in, and some interesting twist to amuse or act out. They may have a pattern and repeated text to support the brain's penchant for repetition and memory. And if the teacher knows what she's doing, she will select the first materials carefully and make sure the reading text has high-frequency one-syllable words that the child is likely to encounter again and again, so that the brain will start picking up on the patterns.

Following Don Holdaway's (1979) and Margaret Mooney's (1990) "big book" recommendations, kindergarten teachers should begin by reading texts *to, with,* and *by* children, as they model the reading of easy material, engage in shared and interactive reading with students, and incorporate echo reading and imitative reading and lots of repetition. Beginning readers memorize, gain confidence, point to the words, get in the flow, and gradually feel like readers—and they are thrilled with the process. At the same time, they begin paying attention to the parts, and in the hands of a knowledgeable teacher, they will be guided to pay attention to particular parts that are important for their development at a particular phase. These concepts Frank Smith had of making reading easy and of learning to read by reading are really very practical.

In 1973 Smith based his understanding of reading on a model of skilled reading. Without the benefit of phase theory, he concluded that "reading may assist writing, but not vice versa" (p. 193). Since then, ample research has shown that spelling and writing at early ages do have a positive impact on reading[1]. Making reference to *mature* writing, Smith warned that it may not assist the child in learning to read due to its "disruptive precepts," such as "correct spelling and grammar, formalized layout, page and paragraph numeration, and neatness of fist" (p. 193). He correctly pointed out that early on, mechanics in mature writing might "interfere chronically with the child's expression of thought" (p. 193). "Apart from anything else, writing is too slow to do anything but interfere with the process of reading," he averred in his exposé of formalized writing and all its accoutrements (p. 193).

Teaching formalized writing along with beginning reading *would* make reading harder because spelling and writing are harder than reading (Bosman & Van Orden, 1997). But what Smith perhaps didn't know in 1973 is that at the beginning levels, "kid writing" (Feldgus & Cardonick, 1997) is *easier* to grasp than reading, is more concrete, and allows the beginner to do exactly what Smith advocated—express his thoughts or meaning in print with confidence and enjoyment. In early writing, the child literally *sees* his thoughts go down on the page while he is thinking about them, and these slow and analytic operations involving the invention of spelling make early writing perfect for beginners because that's how beginners first process print—slowly and analytically (Shaywitz, 2003). "Kid writing" includes all the elements and eventually all the

---

[1] For reading, see Adams, 1990; Chomsky, 1971; Goswami, 1996; Morris, 1981; Strickland, 1998. For writing, see Bissex, 1980; Clay, 1982; Dyson, 1988; Graves, 1978; Sulzby, 1985; Temple, Nathan, & Burris 1982. For spelling, see Bear, Invernizzi, Templeton, & Johnston, 2000; Bolton & Snowball, 1993; Gentry, 1987; Gentry & Gillet, 1993; Wilde, 1992; Zutell, 1999.

parts of conventional writing but is easier for children to accomplish from the start because the conventions and mechanics aren't expected at first. Smith was right on target when he declared that "Children learn to read only by reading" (p. 195). Now we can take a step forward by declaring that children learn to read by writing first *and* reading first. They learn the parts as they use the whole system (Feldgus & Cardonick, 1997).

Beginning reading pedagogy will move forward when we move beyond teaching the parts outside of the system and take advantage of the well-documented fact that many children write *before* they read (Chomsky, 1971). We must make this an instructional advantage. Reading luminaries Donald Durrel and Marie Clay recommended searching for ways to capitalize upon the young child's first urge to write and not to read (Donald Durrel in Graves, 1978, quoted in Clay, 1982). They predicted that for many children, it might be "writing first."

Writing for reading makes sense because invented spelling is the perfect vehicle for code breaking. Writing puts both meaning and phonics first and helps the child synthesize knowledge enabling her to understand how aspects of reading and writing—such as letter knowledge, sound correspondences, directionality, phonemic awareness, phonics and spelling, book concepts, and the concept of "what is a word"—fit together. These are all the dots the child must connect into one grand unified process called reading.

At the beginning level, writing is almost the same as reading. The child writes so that she and perhaps others can *read* what she is thinking. Her purpose in writing is to activate someone's reading circuitry, and in doing it she activates her own reading circuitry. If she asks you, "What did I write?" she's asking you to *read* it back. Sandra Wilde made this connection explicit in a wonderful book titled *You Kan Red This!* (1992). Writing and reading are so intimately connected at the beginning level that they may become impaired when one exists or is presented without the other (Gentry, 2006).

Writing brings a recognized sequence to the child's system of code breaking: first comes writing with no letter knowledge, then with letters but no sounds, then with partial phonemic awareness, then with full, and finally with chunking knowledge (Gentry, 2006). The system follows exactly the same sequence with word reading (Ehri, 1997). Some of the phonics-first experts may hamper the child's likelihood of breaking the code by starting with the segmental nature of words and sounds outside the system. Their notion is that children must first break reading up into parts, separating words into syllables and eventually separating syllables into phonemes (Shaywitz, 2003). But when these activities are delivered outside the system, where is the entry point or child's focus of attention from one activity to the next? We end up with children learning the sounds first, then practicing parts such as phonemes, letters, and sight words. And while some phonics-first advocates pay lip service to writing, spelling, listening, and even playing, imagining, and developing self-confidence (Shaywitz, 2003), too often there is little to guide the teacher in determining when and how one might do these things. There is no sequence or system to it.

Instead of helping children advance through the research-based stages of phase theory, too often we end up with arbitrary "rubrics" and fake scoring systems that have no real connection to what children do in their natural development. For example, some rubrics posit a developmental sequence from "name only" to "words" to "sentences" to "text" (McGill-Franzen, 2006). As you will see in the case studies in Figure 8.9 (see page 98), movement from names to words to sentences to texts may be a logical progression from less sophisticated to more complex elements of text, but beginning writers do not master each of these "parts" in that order. Instead they express their thoughts, and names, words, sentences, and text develop in time, along with formalized aspects of writing and mechanics. The more they write, the more sophisticated their writing gets.

Experts from Marie Clay to Frank Smith have recommended working from the *child's* knowledge base (Clay, 2005; Smith, 1973), attending to what Marie Clay refers to as "child-size concepts of what he's trying to master" (p. 41), but without access to the advances made by phase theory, neither of them recognized a clear sequence for the teacher to follow. Rather, they suggested that every child learns differently. I doubt every child learns to swim, play baseball, ride a bicycle, or eventually drive a car differently, and I doubt reading is learned differently either. The old dictum to try different methods until something works should be canned.

Too often we hear, "Teach the child and not the curriculum" or "Teach children, not methods and materials," but I believe the dichotomy of focusing on the child versus focusing on the method and materials (Smith, 1973) is distorted. One must focus on all of these at the same time:

- Clarify the sequence of code breaking.
- Teach the system of reading and writing.
- Focus on the child and his or her phase level.

- Focus on materials and methods to move the child to the next level.
- Focus on the parts the child is trying to master at a particular phase.
- Direct the child's attention to appropriate parts.

Follow this framework. Focus on the child, the materials, the methods, and the parts at the same time, and phase theory will consolidate and clarify your instruction into one grand unified system.

Focusing on the Phase, the Instruction, the Methods, the Materials, and the Child

It pains me to read that a 5-year-old spent half a year learning to write his name (McGill-Franzen, 2006). Unless there were extenuating circumstances— retardation, visual or hearing impairment, or some catastrophic disability— spending half a year learning to write one's name suggests that the 5-year-old's teachers were watching and waiting but not intervening appropriately. Wouldn't a child become distraught and feel like a failure if he spent half of the kindergarten year learning to write his name? It's not enough to focus on the child—one must help him. One must have some notion of where he is in the sequence, where he's expected to be, what he's paying attention to, and how to direct his attention to move him forward. Without knowing the expected curriculum, it's not possible to work with a child to his advantage. Working with clearly defined phases matched to instruction, methods, and materials is key to improving kindergarten and first-grade pedagogy and moving beyond the spare-parts approach to a universal core curriculum.

Moving Toward Phase Theory and Away From Spare Parts

In her comprehensive book titled *Kindergarten Literacy: Matching Assessment and Instruction in Kindergarten* (2006), Anne McGill-Franzen outlines a model for kindergarten literacy instruction based on the Tennessee Kindergarten Literacy

Project, which sought to correct the gross inconsistencies in kindergarten literacy instruction not only within school districts but sometimes even within the same schools. It was informed by McGill-Franzen's decade of work in and out of kindergarten classrooms. *Kindergarten Literacy* approaches a conceptualization of phase theory through systematic observation of children. Throughout the book, McGill-Franzen recognizes the need for some developmental sequence, affirming that "literacy instruction that is not based on careful observation of individual development will not help all children gain the ground they need to reach their potential" (p. 26). Her search for the phase structure of early development draws from loosely defined developmental spelling stages reported by Bear, Invernizzi, Templeton, & Johnston, 2000.[2] McGill-Franzen recognized Ehri's (1997) stages of word recognition in her discussion of how children develop their knowledge of letters, sounds, and words, and this movement toward a theory of phase development lends credence and power to her vision.

Phase theory replaces loosely defined stages with phases that are precise, straightforward, and systematic. For example, phase theory provides strategic operational definitions for the development of nonreaders, prealphabetic readers, partial alphabetic readers, full alphabetic readers, and chunking readers, as presented in Table 6.1. These precise definitions, identification of specific strategic operations for each level, and identification of expected guideposts for guided reading text levels are critical for matching assessments and instruction in kindergarten and first grade.

Notice that phase theory accommodates formation of guided reading groups at different levels within the same phase. A teacher with ten pupils classified at Phase 2 might create one small guided reading group of Level A text readers and another small guided reading group of children who are managing more sophisticated Level B texts. There is no one-to-one correspondence between phases, stages, and text-leveled reading groups, but there is an expected range of leveled texts that accompanies each phase. It's interesting to note that phase theorists introduce Level A reading texts to both Phase 0 and Phase 1 students at the beginning of kindergarten, earlier than some "spare parts" programs do.

---

[2] Note: I have challenged the accuracy and authenticity of Bear et al. (2000) in a research-based synthesis critiquing stage descriptions in *The Reading Teacher, 54*(3), pp. 318-332.

TABLE 6.1

Phases of Reading Development

	Strategic operations	*Text materials/levels*
Phase 0 Nonreaders	*Readers do not notice letters.* • Name recognition • Recognition of environmental print • Scribbling • Attempted memorization of words and phrases	• Name tags • Labels • Environmental print • LEA charts • Nursery rhyme charts • Picture and poem charts • Caption books, board books • Big books
Phase 1 Prealphabetic readers	*Readers do not use letters.* • Guessing • Cueing from pictures • Using arbitrary cues (golden arches to read *McDonald's*) • Remembering words as visual logo matches for word reading • No systematic letter-sound processing • Attention is paid to nonalphabetic information • Phonological awareness is possible (e.g., clapping syllables, recognizing rhyming words) • No phonemic awareness • Memorization of easy texts	• Name tags • Labels • Environmental print • LEA charts • Adult underwriting • Nursery rhyme charts • Picture and poem charts • Big books • Keep books, caption books, pattern books, alphabet books, pop-up books, board books, concept books (animals, colors, numbers, plants, shapes, and so on) *Probable reading level begins with environmental print, names, words, labels, and phrases and moves on to a few Level A easy books.*

Breakthrough in Beginning Reading and Writing

TABLE 6.1 Phases of Reading Development (*continued*)

	Strategic operations	*Text materials/levels*
Phase 2 Partial alphabetic readers	*Readers cue on beginning and ending letters and sounds.* • Form partial letter-sound representations • Pay little or no attention to medial vowels • Match some letters to sounds • Rely on rudimentary alphabet knowledge • Start using the voice-to-print match • Echo reading • Text memorization of Level A to Level C easy text • Rereading adult underwriting or LEA stories	• Adult underwriting • Nursery rhyme charts • Picture and poem charts • Big books • Keep books, pattern books, alphabet books, pop-up books, board books, concept books (animals, colors, numbers, plants, shapes, and so on) *Probable reading level is Level A to C easy books. Phase 2 readers greatly increase the number of books they can read from memory. By cueing on partial alphabetic information, they memorize text more easily than Phase 1 readers do.*
Phase 3 Full alphabetic readers	*Readers cue on full word reading by paying attention to all the letters in words.* • Sound words out letter by letter i-n-t-e-r-e-s-t-i-n-g (e.g., don't recognize chunks: in-ter-est-ing) • Pay attention to medial vowels • Match letters to sounds • Display full phonemic awareness • Analogize using word families	• Adult underwriting is dropped • Children read own writing as it is created • Fiction and nonfiction *Probable reading level is Level C to Level H. Phase 3 readers greatly increase the number of books they can read and flourish in material that helps them learn medial vowel patterns (especially CVC short vowels), word families, and chunks of phonics patterns for pattern recognition.*

TABLE 6.1 Phases of Reading Development (*continued*)

	Strategic operations	*Text materials/levels*
Phase 3 (*continued*)	• Greatly increase store of sight words • Decode new words, letter by letter • Use grapheme-to-sound cues extensively • Echo reading continues • Text memorization continues • Ability to decode increases	
Phase 4 Chunking Readers	*Readers chunk in phonics patterns or recognize high-frequency one-syllable words as chunks in polysyllabic words—for example,* dig *and* in *in* indignation. • More words are processed automatically rather than slowly and analytically from chunking letter-sound representations. • Sense themselves as grown-up readers • Decode nonsense words— *dit, buf, fler* • Use chunks for graphosyllabic analysis • Less dependent on word walls for new vocabulary • Learn new vocabulary by reading independently • Read independently without the need to memorize text through repeated readings	• Fiction and nonfiction *Probable reading level is Level J to K or higher, including chapter books. Reading is much more proficient and fluent than it was at previous levels.*

Writing for Reading and Moving Away From Spare Parts

Teachers who teach writing from the beginning report remarkable progress in kindergarten literacy programs. I sent two award-winning kindergarten teachers who have writing-driven reading programs the hypothetical case study presented below to get a sense of their real-life expectations. These extraordinary teachers, who operate classrooms based in phase theory, sent back the responses below.

Gentry's Hypothetical Case

A child enters your kindergarten classroom at the beginning of the year at Phase 0. He can't write his name and he doesn't know the letters or sounds of the alphabet. This child speaks English as his native language. You do what you do. By midyear he identifies sounds for only ten letters, has no letter-sound correspondence, and can write only his name and the word *I*. By the end of the year he identifies all upper-and lowercase letters, provides the appropriate sounds for 23 letters, and he is reading on Level A. Based on your experience, how would you assess his progress?

Isabell Cardonick, Philadelphia

I would expect more progress. When children are exposed to writing from Day 1 (even children who don't know the alphabet when they first enter school), they generally learn the entire alphabet within the first few months of school—because they are using the letters as needed in their writing rather than focusing only on "a letter a week" as is done in some classrooms. In my classroom, I don't have the children simply label their pictures—even at the beginning of the year, they write "stories" in whole sentences about their pictures. So I would not have them memorize labels, but would teach them how to use print in the classroom to support their story or nonfiction writing. Children quickly learn the words used most

In my classroom, I don't have the children simply label their pictures—even at the beginning of the year, they write "stories" in whole sentences about their pictures.

::

frequently in writing. I would also begin doing shared reading with Level A books, highlighting (with highlighting tape) the same high-frequency words the children are using in their writing. These same words are also placed on the word wall, and they receive repeated exposure through teacher modeling and repeated use in interactive writing experiences such as morning messages and story retellings.

In Philadelphia, the reading benchmark for the end of kindergarten is instructional level D. In my classroom, most children are able to move far beyond this goal. Looking at a sample end-of-year assessment from my classroom in 2005–06, I see that 16 out of 30 children were reading at instructional levels G through K. The lowest-achieving children generally reach instructional level C. There are usually about 3 to 5 children out of 30 at this lowest level. [Isabell Cardonick is coauthor with Eileen Feldgus of *Kid Writing: A Systematic Approach to Phonics, Journals, and Writing Workshop* (1999).]

Paula Paulos, Dallas

I would not consider the hypothetical case "awesome achievement," though it does definitely show progress. I never delay students' independent writing; to the contrary, I encourage it from the very beginning of kindergarten! In our fifth week of school, I have students drawing, adding detail to their drawings, labeling pictures with beginning sounds, using consonant frameworks, creating phonetic spellings such as SAL for *sail* and RAN for *rain*, and writing in phrases and sentences at their developmental spelling levels or the phase level where they are capable. We begin this process in our second week of school, which is our first week of the full-day schedule. With my teacher modeling in the morning message, mini-lessons in writing workshop, and frequent use of Elkonin boxes, my students are able to jump into writing, and they are well on their way! First I assess letter/sound knowledge, then I do running records to determine instructional reading levels. The process takes *forever* in kindergarten! By September this year, I already knew that I had a range from very limited letter knowledge to letter mastery. Within that first month, I determined that my class ranged from nonreaders to perhaps first- or second-grade reading levels. I had a few students that could not write their names when they entered kindergarten.

None of this baseline data interferes with learning all of the aspects of beginning literacy that grow out of our joyful reading and writing both in concert and in context.

In my classroom, writing drives reading, and all of my students are expected to leave kindergarten reading at a minimum of reading level C/D. Many of my students reach higher levels. So far I'm meeting my goals, and it gets better every year as I learn more and more from my students of what they are capable of achieving!

Describing assessment of text reading in *Kindergarten Literacy*, Anne McGill-Franzen provides a useful and concise synthesis of the value of writing for reading:

In my classroom, writing drives reading, and all of my students are expected to leave kindergarten reading at a minimum of reading level C/D. Many of my students reach higher levels.

::

> **Reads Back Writing:** *This is often the first actual—conventional— reading a child does. It is the easiest text for a child to read because it comes from him—both ideas and the printed message that communicates the ideas. The child draws a picture to represent what he is thinking, then uses what he knows about letters, sounds, words, and print concepts to create a written text that explains his drawing. By looking at his writing . . . we can see what he knows about words.*
>
> *If a child is able to read back his own writing, saying, for example, the same word whenever he sees a particular combination of letters, or reading the text back in exactly the same way, regardless of how often you ask him to do it, he is demonstrating the same principle: words are invariant. Being able to read back writing is actual reading—the child points to each word, making a voice-print match; he uses initial letters to help support his memory for words; he uses the drawing he created to support his memory for the ideas he wishes to communicate. (p. 102)*

Not much needs to be added to this statement, except perhaps to explain that if adult underwriting is added at the bottom of the page in the same word order and line arrangement as the child created, the child will read back her own writing *cueing from conventional text*, which enables even higher levels of reading.

Early writing is powerful for reading. Much of what teachers measure in spare-parts assessments may be observed and recorded quite easily from observations of what beginners do in their writing. Not only does phase theory cut back on testing time, paperwork, assessments, and drills, it reveals the system and the sequence and pulls all the spare parts together into one unified operational system.

CHAPTER 7

Shifts in Reading Recovery

Phase theory supports a shift in our thinking about early intervention models such as Reading Recovery, developed by the late Marie Clay. In her last Reading Recovery manual and manifesto on beginning-reading intervention, Clay (2005a) noted shifts in our thinking that are already happening; she made a cogent analogy between reading instruction and recent groundbreaking changes in early mathematics instruction:

> Almost nobody considering the young child learning beginning mathematics is going to think in terms of how many arithmetical items he knows. Almost everybody will be thinking: "What mathematical operations can he carry out?" Although we may not yet have definitive descriptions of all the strategic activities or operations that are acquired in early literacy, this kind of shift in our thinking is happening. (p. 13)

Phase theory offers those definitive descriptions, clarifying the precise phase sequence, the type and timing of instruction, and a natural step-by-step progression for beginning readers and writers. The monitoring of these early, easy-to-recognize phases is so precise that teachers are now able to identify problems in development, recognize lack of preparation for success with literacy, and provide early intervention a full year before Reading Recovery begins. While strict adherents to Reading Recovery are still waiting for low achievers to be identified in first grade, teachers who understand phase theory are taking action to prevent failure and providing joyful, age-appropriate, child-friendly teaching and intervention in kindergarten.

There are few contemporary reading researchers whom I hold in higher regard than Marie Clay. Her brilliant research and body of work in literacy education are unparalleled in the last half century. But in light of phase theory, Clay's latest work must withstand new scrutiny and, I believe, the general theory of learning to read and write that underlies Reading Recovery must undergo extensive change. Let me be specific:

1. The Reading Recovery establishment must embrace a natural dichotomy between beginning readers and skilled readers and abandon the theory that led us astray for one hundred years, during which time we based our observations on the notion that the beginner reads like the skilled reader. This shift in perspective will require teachers to adjust observations and thinking away from "good readers" versus "slow readers," away from "high-progress readers" versus "low-progress readers," and away from the implication that we have "sick readers who must recover." The shift is away from a notion that many children in the second year of schooling are "the hardest-to-teach-children" (Clay, 2005a, p. i) and toward the recognition that most of these children simply come to us in the first year as healthy learners who are underprepared for literacy success in kindergarten. We must abandon descriptions of children as "intractable," "hard to distinguish," and "not responding well" and embrace the notion that most of them "would do well if they got the resources" they needed soon enough (David Pearson quoted in Clay, 2005, p. 15). The adjustment must include observation and progress monitoring of the phases and natural strategic operations that are acquired in early literacy for breaking the code.

2. Reading Recovery must stop suggesting that all beginning readers learn differently (and therefore need individual attention delivered by an elite force of specially trained teachers) and recognize that most readers learn the same way and travel the same path. And while the teachers who teach beginning readers have to be immersed in thoughtful professional development, the course of study should be available for everyone, not relegated to a privileged few. Once we have a core curriculum recognizing phase observation and phase monitoring, a uniform beginning reading curriculum, which borrows liberally from Reading Recovery training and reading-for-meaning theory, should be established much like the basic anatomy core curriculum in medical schools. Not to provide this kind of professional development for *all* American teachers of beginning reading is unconscionable.

3. The Reading Recovery establishment must move beyond the conflict over decoding emphasis and meaning emphasis theories resulting in the reading wars that have held progress in reading education at bay for over a century. All reading scholars must abandon Clay's (2005a) assumption "that a theory of reading continuous texts cannot arise from a theory of word reading" (p. 19). The two are absolutely compatible in light of phase theory and new understandings of reading and writing reciprocity. Linnea Ehri's theory of word reading (Ehri, 1992, 1997, and 1998), the parallel developmental spelling theory (Gentry, 1985, 2004, 2006; Henderson, 1990; Morris, Bloodgood, Lomax, & Perney, 2003; Templeton & Bear, 1992), and much of the theory supported in Clay's view of reading acquisition (Clay, 1982, 1991, 1998, 2001, 2005a, 2005b, and 2005c) are stronger when fused than they are in isolation and opposition.

4. The Reading Recovery establishment must embrace the practice of delivering instruction in set sequences of natural development. The responses of most children in learning to read are not "extremely different" as supposed by many Reading Recovery proponents (Clay, 2005a, p. 21). In most instances teachers need not "be able to detect how different the path has to be for individual children" (Clay, p. 10) because for most children, the path is the same. What happens to 5-year-old children who come into the first classes in schools is that they move naturally and progressively through five developmental phases necessary for breaking the code. With appropriate teaching, teachers "can shift children from one level of competence and sophistication to the next" (Clay, p. 8). Recall our five phases—the sequence of operations that normal developing readers and writers carry out:

    Operating Without Letter Knowledge (Phase 0)

    Operating With Letters but Without Sounds (Phase 1)

    Operating With Partial Phonemic Awareness (Phase 2)

What happens to 5-year-old children who come into the first classes in schools is that they move naturally and progressively through five developmental phases necessary for breaking the code.

::

Operating With Full Phonemic Awareness (Phase 3)

Operating With Full Code and Chunking Knowledge (Phase 4)

Attention to these phases will completely revamp literacy education, Reading Recovery, and early intervention and will provide precision and accuracy in early literacy instruction. Early literacy problems can be solved with a good curriculum based on these natural phases of development and implemented by well-trained teachers who do many of the things that Reading Recovery teachers do, in a child-friendly environment. Additionally, we must pay more attention to preschool environments so that children arrive in the first year of school prepared for success with literacy.

5.   The Reading Recovery establishment must abandon the egregious practice of waiting until first grade to intervene with students who are having difficulty. Clay (2005a) writes, "We now know that we can pick out the children at about six years of age who do not have effective control of beginning reading and writing behaviors that other children have learned" (p. 10).

Paying attention to phase development doesn't mean that we teach all children the same. We teach into their phases and their natural development as writers and readers.

::

This is too late for the millions of children who come to school perfectly capable of learning but underprepared for reading and writing due to a lack of literacy exposure from infancy to age 4. All children should enter kindergarten writing their own name and singing the alphabet song. English language learners must be exposed to English vocabulary and English spelling patterns from the start if we plan to test their English writing skills in fourth grade. Learning to read in Spanish, for example, may transfer to proficient third-grade reading in English but not to proficient writing unless Spanish speakers are taught the complex English spelling code. Writing is harder than reading and requires more word-specific knowledge. (Fourth graders can read novels, but how many can write them?)

One of the greatest strengths of Reading Recovery is clearly stated in italics by Clay (2005a) in the her last Reading Recovery manifesto: she fully recognized that the teacher must understand "a theory of what the child must learn to attend to and how he must work with print as he reads and writes" (p. 30). This statement is precisely what phase theory is all about. Where Clay and Reading Recovery falter is in Clay's belief that all children learn differently. She admonishes,

> With problem readers it is not enough for the teacher to have rapport, to generate interesting tasks and generally be a good teacher. The teacher must be able to design a superbly sequenced series of lessons determined by the particular child's competencies, and make highly skilled decisions moment by moment during the lesson . . . An expert teacher will help the child to leap appropriately; she will not walk the child through a preconceived sequence of learning step by step. (Clay, 2005a, p. 23)

Indeed, beginning reading teachers must include in their work a design for a superbly sequenced series of differentiated lessons. But these should be based on the five phases—a wonderfully natural, step-by-step sequence of learning. Teachers of beginning reading and writing, among other things, must recognize the phases of code breaking. They must know the accomplishments generally expected at certain points in time in the first two years of schooling. They must not wait until first grade for intervention; intervention must begin earlier.

In my view, this is a flaw in Reading Recovery that needs fixing. Why must we *wait* before we shift children from one level of confidence to another, wait before we pay attention to the criteria for moving children forward? If "the observation procedures identify the children who need help and they show where the areas of strength and weakness lie" (Clay, 2005a, p. 12), observation must start long before first grade. Paying attention to phase development doesn't mean that we teach all children in the same way. We teach into their phases and their natural development as writers and readers. Phase monitoring is a splendid way to know when progress is not occurring from the very beginning. It is a splendid way to differentiate instruction.

Clay (2005a) writes,

> What could be achieved if some rather different supplementary instruction were available for a young learner who was clearly not able to keep up with his classmates after one year at school? Suppose the system provided, for a short period of time, an individual treatment, somewhat analogous to medical intensive care. It would occur every day and be tailored to the learner's particular need. (p. 17)

Must we wait a year for readers to get "sick," so that we can identify the ones who need help? Wouldn't a better solution be earlier intervention? Can we practice preventive medicine?

In my work with teachers, I am often impressed by the confidence and fine work of Reading Recovery teachers. "I didn't really know how to teach beginning reading before my training in Reading Recovery," they tell me. "Now I know how to teach reading!" There is much to be praised and gleaned from the fine model of Reading Recovery. But the winds of reading education, even as noted by Clay, have shifted. Earlier intervention is a necessity. Reading Recovery must change.

CHAPTER 8

One Clear Path

"You don't see what you're seeing until you see it," Dr. Thurston
said, *"but when you do see it, it lets you see many other things."*
(Overbye, 2006)

Dr. William Thurston's quote is about an elusive mathematical proof of a
famous problem about the nature of space posed by the French polymath
Henri Poincaré in 1904. When a Russian mathematician, Grigory Perelman,
reported that he had solved the problem in 2003, the whole scientific
community embraced the discovery with excitement. It led to other insights.
When a teacher sees the clear path of phase observation, the effect is the same.
It may seem simple, but it allows one to see everything differently. I believe
phase theory is allowing for deep connections in literacy theory that weren't
thought of or capable of being proven previously, such as the intricate
connections of beginning-reading and -writing reciprocity and the compatibility
of meaning-based and code-emphasis stances. Seeing one clear path in
beginning literacy changes everything.

The invention of instruments has lead to new knowledge and paradigm shifts
in reading. The microscope and scientific study of eye movements helped Edmund
B. Huey form his theories about skilled reading in 1908, theories that greatly
informed psychology, linguistics, and the psycholinguistics of reading. Now it is
the computer and functioning magnetic resonance imaging, or fMRI, that is
making possible the latest advance.

New computer technology using PET (positron emission tomography) brain scans and fMRI has allowed neuroscientists to discover basic neural pathways for reading, leading to new understandings of dyslexia. Using computers and magnets not only to get high-contrast images of the brain but also to determine which constellations of neurons are firing off during cognitive processes such as reading has enabled some neuroscientists to begin creating a reading map of the brain by charting the neural circuitry for reading (Shaywitz, 2003, reported in Gentry, 2006). In a nutshell, here's what some neuroscientists are saying: Most normal readers have a left hemisphere reading system with three major areas activated for skilled reading. For the sake of simplicity, let's call these major reading areas A, B, and C, as shown in Figure 8.1, and speculate on when and how each of these areas might be activated in the beginning reading classroom.

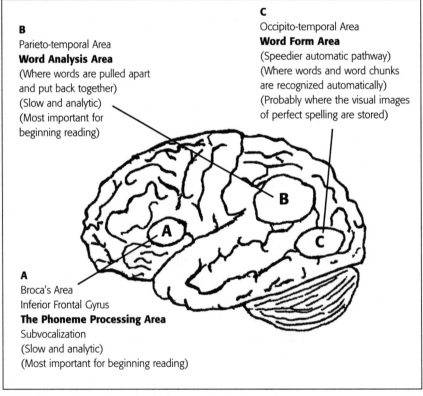

C
Occipito-temporal Area
Word Form Area
(Speedier automatic pathway)
(Where words and word chunks
are recognized automatically)
(Probably where the visual images
of perfect spelling are stored)

B
Parieto-temporal Area
Word Analysis Area
(Where words are pulled apart
and put back together)
(Slow and analytic)
(Most important for
beginning reading)

A
Broca's Area
Inferior Frontal Gyrus
The Phoneme Processing Area
Subvocalization
(Slow and analytic)
(Most important for beginning reading)

FIGURE 8.1 Left Hemisphere Brain Systems for Reading

Area A, the "phoneme processing area," might be activated when a kindergarten teacher has children shout out the rhyming word in a nursery rhyme

Breakthrough in Beginning Reading and Writing

as they repeat in unison: "Jack and Jill went up the *hill*." As Shaywitz reports in *Overcoming Dyslexia*, this area is slow and analytical and most likely to be used in the beginning stages of learning to read (p. 81). This corroborates the known importance of phonological processing and phonemic awareness in the beginning stages of learning to read as well as hundreds of years of conventional wisdom acknowledging the benefit of nursery rhymes.

Area B is a specific neural site identified by Shaywitz and others as the area responsible for word analysis or sounding out words and, I believe, the beginning phases of invented spelling. It's where words are pulled apart and put back together. If a first-grade teacher is having children "finger spell" a word like *rat* at the beginning of first grade (sticking up the thumb for the /r/ sound, holding out the pointer finger for the /ă/ sound, sticking out the third finger for the /t/ sound, then reaching out and "grabbing" the sounds to pull them back into the word as she and the children repeat together, "/r/, /ă/, /t/, *rat!*"), then the children are likely activating Area B. Shaywitz (2003) describes Area B this way: "Slow and analytic, its function seems to be in the early stages of learning to read, that is, in initially analyzing a word, pulling it apart, and linking its letters to their sounds" (p. 79). I would describe Areas A and B as being most important during the "tadpole" reading and writing phases.

Area C is what Shaywitz (2003) calls the "word form" area, and its activation leads to the "express pathway to reading" (p. 79). Activation of this area, for most normal skilled readers, is basic for recognizing words automatically and perhaps for visual recognition and recall of spelling patterns (Gentry, 2004).

Because the brain processes information by searching for patterns (Brynes, 2001), the pattern the skilled reader is attending to is likely spelling chunks such as those that make up most one-syllable, high-frequency words. Phase theorists posit that once children know enough high-frequency sight words—such as *dig* and *in*—and once they have knowledge of phonics chunks, they can *see* the regular patterns in printed English and recognize them automatically (Gentry, 2004, 2006). The mapping of print-to-spoken language in English likely includes not only letter-to-sound but also chunk-to-chunk mapping. So Area C may be completely activated once children recognize enough sight words and have enough word-specific and chunking knowledge to see the patterns in print automatically. Activation of Area C, the speedier pathway, allows children eventually to process new words after a few repeated exposures in meaningful context. Thus first-grade-level word-wall work resulting in automatic recognition of *dig* and *in* might be the precursor to later automatic recognition of these same syllable chunks in the word *indignation*. Such automatic word processing and eventual recognition of chunks of phonics patterns allow the "tadpole" reader to go beyond the beginning slow and analytical processes of attending to letters and sounds and use higher-level interactive processes. Instead of memorizing and decoding words, they begin attending to more sophisticated, meaning-driven levels of language processing such as semantics, syntax, and activation of the basic neural sites for speaking and understanding language. After the code is broken, much of the word recognition and decoding becomes automatic. It has been well documented that the upper levels of language processing are important for skilled reading, during which the reader constructs meaning as his eyes dance across the page. Skilled reading is not really word pronouncing—it's "thought getting" (Huey, 1908, p. 349). Beginning versus proficient is a change from slow and analytical to automatic—from beginning early phases to skilled mature reading, from "tadpole" to "frog" reading. Eventually the slow and analytical decoding process gives way to a more complex, automatic meaning-based process.

So why didn't someone notice this before now? It seems simple: *Beginning reading is different from skilled reading.* Well, someone did. . . .

Between the years 1962 and 1965, while a professor at City College of the City University of New York, Dr. Jeanne Chall, who would later teach at the Harvard Graduate School of Education, identified the distinction between beginning and mature reading in the conclusion of her landmark 1967 book, *Learning to Read: The Great Debate.* Funded by a grant from the Carnegie Corporation, Chall had interviewed the reading luminaries of the mid-twentieth century, examined the existing research base, painstakingly analyzed conflicting methods of teaching beginning reading, observed beginning reading classrooms in both the United States and Great Britain, and finally endorsed the phonics-first position. This monumental investigation began with one germane question: "What is the best way to teach a young child to read?" (p. 1), and in the end, Chall made the beginning-versus-skilled reading distinction. In addition, she recommended emphasizing code over meaning. Chall averred that research from 1912 to 1965 backed a code-emphasis approach. I believe her most brilliant finding was her declaration that code emphasis "views *beginning reading as essentially different from mature reading*" (p. 307, emphasis added). Forty-five years later, fMRIs would supply the proof.

Seeing the Phases in One Clear Path

Much that is important about phase observation is seeing the natural path of development in a sequence of phases that is essentially different from mature reading. Once the teacher recognizes each beginning phase, she must adjust the type and timing of instruction to what a child is paying attention to at a particular phase. Marie Clay's own words, which I have taken out of context, describe phase theory exactly: it is *"a theory of what the child must learn to attend to and how he must work with print as he reads and writes"* (Clay, 2005a, p. 30). Yet phase theory is driven by what happens naturally when children use primitive writing in a desire to express themselves. By observing the clear path of phase theory—the natural scheme of writing and reading development—and by adjusting instruction to what the beginning reader's brain is paying attention to at a particular point in time, teachers can move children forward step by step, and they can see when a child is not progressing as expected. Remarkably, they can provide exactly the type of instruction the child needs to move to the next level.

The beauty of seeing the phases of beginning reading and writing in one clear path is its simplicity. As the mathematician said, "when you do see it, it lets you see many other things." I have to admit that I looked at developmental stages of spelling for almost thirty years before I understood the implications of what I was seeing in terms of the beginnings of literacy. What I saw as stages of spelling development were the phases of beginning writing and reading. Others—namely Henderson (1990), Ehri (1997), Bodrova and Leong (1998), and Silva and Alves-Martins (2002)— showed me, though I don't think they fully appreciated the importance of it either. But as Dr. Thurston pointed out, "you don't see what you're seeing until you see it."

In the section that follows, we look at various children in the process of breaking the code and see how code breaking works. Some are children developing as expected, and some show unbalanced and stymied development. Yet all of these children follow the same path to code breaking. One child whose samples are presented was the precocious child of a Harvard researcher whose mother tracked his learning from 4 to 6 years of age (Bissex, 1980). Two others are the children of reading teachers who joyfully engaged in reading and writing from infancy. Another smart child (now a medical doctor) had supportive experiences at home but lacked early writing experience or phonics instruction in school and became a victim of an unbalanced approach. While he excelled as a reader, he struggled with spelling and writing, which were not taught formally. In January of his first-grade year his mother brought him to a university reading clinic to address his "writing disability," even though he was a reading above grade level. His writing samples show his advancement through three phases in sixteen weeks after appropriate early intervention in the clinic (Gentry, 1987).

In all cases, we see strategic operations for code breaking unfolding in children naturally. Victims of too much phonics and not enough writing are not shown, because children who aren't allowed to write leave no record of their phase progress or lack of advancement. Could the thousands of children subjected to No Child Left Behind's insidious "Reading First" policy, which dictates "reading only" in 90-minute blocks and disallows writing, be included in this group? Some of these children may be stifled as readers as well.

As we look at the one clear path in the samples that follow, keep in mind that once one sees the step-by-step sequence and knows what the child is paying attention to at each phase, one can provide instruction that fits the phase. One can help beginners move forward along a common path, and one can know with assurance when children aren't progressing as expected. Powerfully, if the child isn't advancing, one will know what to do about it.

Seeing Phase 0—Operations Without Letter Knowledge

A period of operating with no letter knowledge is expected before children enter kindergarten. Look at the samples of writing in Figure 8.2, and let's determine the writers' strategic operation and what these samples of children's writing have in common.

At 2 years, 4 months of age, Meredith (now an adult) scribbled a message on a greeting card (Gentry, 1987). Antonio turned in his "writing" to his kindergarten teacher (Gentry, 2004). Horatio produced a sample that says "Happy People" in a kindergarten writing workshop in September (Gentry, 2006). At 2 years, 6 months of age, Leslie sent an Easter card to her grandmother (Gentry and Gillet, 1993). Three-year-old Amy spelled the words *monster*, *united*, and *dress*, with straight lines after admitting that she cannot write her name. This easily identified phase is unmistakable. It is what every child does when he or she is given pen and paper and encouraged to write before he or she can write his or her name. All of these writers have the same strategic operation: they scribble, represent writing with a straight line, have no recognizable letters, do squiggly marks, or they do wavy or loopy writing with differing orientations on the page. These children are in Phase 0. They are writers who do not use letters.

(A)

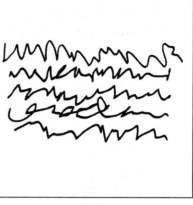

(B)

(C)

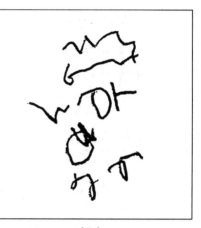

(D)

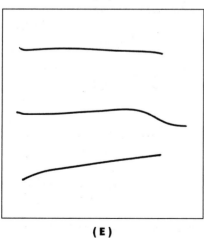

(E)

FIGURE 8.2 Phase 0 Writing

(A) Meredith's scribbled message on a greeting card:
     2 years, 4 months old

(B) Antonio's nonalphabetic writing:
     Kindergarten (September)

(C) Horatio's "Happy People"

(D) Leslie's scribbled message on a greeting card:
     2 years, 6 months old

(E) Amy's Monster Test

Breakthrough in Beginning Reading and Writing

Whether Phase 0 happens at 2 years and 4 months of age or in the first month of kindergarten, Phase 0 is extraordinarily revealing: it says, this child is interested in writing. But when legions of children enter kindergarten at Phase 0, they are already in line for failure due to lack of preparation. They already need special intervention. We must teach them to write and read their names.

Seeing Phase 1—Operations With Letters but Without Sounds

Look at the samples of writing in Figure 8.3, and let's determine the writers' strategic operation or what these samples of children's writing have in common.

FIGURE 8.3 Phase 1 Writing

(A) Paul's writing: 4 years old (B) Meredith's scribbling and letters on a greeting card: 3 years, 5 months old (C) Dan's grocery list (D) Leslie's writing

Breakthrough in Beginning Reading and Writing

Meredith signs a greeting card to be sent to her grandmother combining scribbling and letters at age 3 years, 5 months. At 4 years of age, Paul writes a "Welcome Home" banner (Bissex, 1980). Five-year-old Dan makes a grocery list: "*7Up, milk, Raisin Bran, doughnuts*" (Gentry, 1987). At 3 years of age, Leslie moves beyond attempts to write her name and describes her drawing of "a flock of butterflies" with a string of random *l*'s, *e*'s, *m*'s, *i*'s, *n*'s, *d*'s, and *r*'s (Gentry & Gillet, 1993). All of these writers use the same strategic operation for these Phase 1 spellings. The writing appears as letters but the letters do not correspond to the words' sounds. These children may need intervention if they have moved beyond the middle of kindergarten.

Seeing Phase 2—Operations With Partial Phonemic Awareness

Let's look at the samples of writing in Figure 8.4 and determine the writers' strategic operation or what these samples of children's writing have in common.

Paul writes "RUDF" "Are you deaf?" at 5 years, 1 month of age. (Bissex, 1980; Gentry, 1987). When "Daddy" sneaks a cocktail, 5-year-old Meredith reports the activity to her mother in a picture and writing: "Daddy pouring a drink" (Gentry, 1982). In February of his first-grade year, Dan writes about what he would do with magic. Leslie writes "HMT DPD" "Humpty Dumpty" just as she turns 6 years old (Gentry & Gillet, 1993).While demonstrating a range of writing quantity and different levels of reading and word knowledge, all of these writers use the same

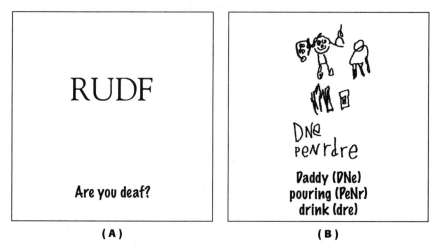

FIGURE 8.4 Phase 2 Writing

(A) Paul's writing: 5 years, 1 month old (B) Meredith's writing: 5 years old

(C)   **(D)**

FIGURE 8.4 Phase 2 Writing *(CONTINUED)*

(C) Dan's writing: first grade (February)   (D) Leslie's "Humpty Dumpty": 6 years

strategic operation for inventing Phase 2 spellings. They are operating with partial alphabetic knowledge. Even Dan, who reads at second-grade level, leaves out some sounds when inventing most of the unknown spellings in his story about magic, such as CRTS for *karats*, CLFFORD for *Clifford*, CAMR for *camera*, BASKBALL for *basketball*, and LBRTE for *liberty*. Dan likely had already activated some higher-level processes for reading, perhaps using semantic and syntactic cues to drive the reading process, and he already had a large sight-word vocabulary. But unlike some children who break the code on their own with this level of functioning, there were gaps in Dan's understanding of the how the code worked, and he was unable to consolidate the whole reading/writing process. This somewhat idiosyncratic case left this good reader stymied as a writer. Phase 2 spelling is expected by the end of kindergarten.

Seeing Phase 3—Operations With Full Phonemic Awareness

Now, let's turn to the samples of writing in Figure 8.5 and determine the writers' strategic operation or what these samples of children's writing have in common.

At 5 years 2 months of age, in wonderful Phase 3 writing, Paul expresses himself: "EF U KAN OPN KAZ I WIL GEV U A KN OPENR," "If you can open cans I will give you a can opener." Paul types in one letter for each sound in every word (except KN) (Bissex, 1980; Gentry, 2006). Meredith is greatly impressed by a car-safety film she views showing what happens to a mannequin that's not

Breakthrough in Beginning Reading and Writing

EF U KAN OPN KAZ I WILL
GEV U A KN OPENR

If you can open cans I will give
you a can opener

(A)

SAFte
AN A CAt
et SCHod A
MAN ACN. ef et
deaNt HAV
ON els set
aN! BLt et
Wtd FOL
FU VA WNdo

(B)

TAS-AS—E-PAO
RR-FER-MOM—
I-HEPUOU
LEK-TAS
@ PACH
ERR-EV
DNL DEF
AND DAS
Y DEC.

(C)

my oll truck
My truck is gray.
My truck shuts wAter
out. on the side it ses
MobOl. It rais and Jumps rdmps
It's block) blue, red and
white. I pldy weth it.

(D)

FIGURE 8.5 Phase 3 Writing

(A) Paul's writing: 5 years, 2 months old (B) Meredith's safety film critique: 5 years, 3 months
old (C) Leslie's "Donald and Daisy": 6 years, 3 months old (D) Dan's writing: first grade (March)

strapped in with a seatbelt. She entitles it "Safety in a Car" and she writes a
synopsis: "It showed a mannequin. If it didn't have on its seat belt, it would fall
through the window" (Gentry, 1987). At 6 years, 3 months of age Leslie writes
about Donald and Daisy Duck: "This is a picture for Mom. I hope you like this
picture of Donald Duck and Daisy Duck" (13 of the 18 invented spellings are
Phase 3) (Gentry & Gillet, 1993). At about the same age, she wrote to the tooth
fairy: TUTH FARE. WN NIT I WS N MI bed and the TUTH FARE CAM.
(Gentry & Gillet, 1993). In the first week of March of first grade, Dan wrote a
wonderful story about his oil truck: "My OLL truck. My truck is gray. My truck

SHUTS water out. On the side it SES MOBOL. It ROLS and jumps ramps. It's black, blue, red and white. I play WETH it." (Gentry, 1987) He invents five of the misspelled words with a letter for each sound, which is Phase 3. While these samples contain an occasional Phase 2 or Phase 4 spelling, the vast majority of the invented spellings are rendered with one letter for each sound in the word. These Phase 3 writers demonstrate full phonemic awareness. They all use the same strategic operation, which is full alphabetic spelling in which a letter is present for each sound in the word except when the word has special sound features that "carry" the sound, such as preconsonantal nasals, syllabic *r*'s, and sonorant *l*'s or *n*'s as in MOSTR for *monster*, WITR for *weather*, and MANACN for *mannequin*, respectively. Phase 3 is expected by the middle of first grade.

Figure 8.7 illustrates specific sound features that researchers have found to be spelled phonetically at Phase 3, showing the complexity and perceptual accuracy of these children's creative spelling.

Seeing Phase 4—Operations With Full Code and Chunking Knowledge

Look at the samples of writing in Figure 8.6, and let's determine the writers' strategic operation or what these samples of children's writing have in common.

At 6 years 1 month of age, Paul demonstrates a chunking system for writing in English even though he hasn't learned all the conventional chunks. He writes a weather forecast and news report such as "THES AFTERNEWN it's going to rain. It's going to be fair TOMORO" and "FAKTARE'S (factories) can no longer OFORD making play DOW (doh)" (Bissex, 1980). Notice unconventional chunks for words such as THES for *this*, NEWN for *noon*, TOMORO for *tomorrow*, FAKTARE'S for *factories*, OFORD for *afford*, and DOW as in *low* for *doh*. Meredith's autobiographical sketch says, "My Baby Story. I was born on January the 4. I got born at 5-0-10. I weighed around 1 pound. The first time I went to Winston-Salem, I did a stinky in my Mom's lap. I ate ham and green beans mixed. I wore a white dress with lace on it." Notice her move into Phase 4 with chunking spellings, many of which are influenced by her rather prominent Southern dialect such as BABE for *baby*, BAON for *born*, JANURRE for *January*, WAOD for *weighed*, FARST for *first*, AT for *it*, DEAD for *did*, WIET for *white*, and WETH for *with* (Gentry, 1987). In May of his first grade year, Dan traced an outline of his foot on a piece of writing paper and wrote a piece that he called "My Foot." (This had followed a piece that he had entitled "My Penis," which shocked us a bit until we discovered he was writing about his penny collection!) Not so shocking but equally wonderful is the next

FIGURE 8.6 Phase 4 Writing

(A) Paul's writing: 6 years, 1 month old (B) Meredith's autobiographical story: 6 years, 5 months old (C) Dan's writing: first grade (May) (D) Phase 4 spelling

piece, a second grader's description of things she likes to eat. In all of these samples the writers use the same strategic operation, which is to spell in chunks of phonics patterns. Here's where spelling gets really interesting, with myriad possibilities, a few of which are listed in Figure 8.8 for your pleasure. What's not so amusing is to see these same spellings in the writing of seventh and eighth graders, which happens too often in schools where spelling books have been eliminated and teaching spelling is considered old-fashioned (Gentry, 2005). Phase 4 spelling is expected by the end of first grade.

FIGURE 8.7

8 Sound Features With Phase 3 Spellings

Sound feature	What It Means	Sample Word	Phase 3 Spelling
tense vowels	long-vowel sound	eighty eat ice oak you	AT (letter name) ET IC OK U
lax vowels	short-vowel sound	bat bet bit cot cut	BUT (vowel shift) BAT BET CIT COT
preconsonantal nasal	n or m before a consonant	jump stamp	JUP STAP
syllabic sonorants	l, m, or n carries the vowel sound in a syllable	bottle atom open	BOTL ATM OPN
-ed endings	past-tense marker	stopped dimmed traded	STOPT DIMD TRADAD
retroflex vowels	r-controlled vowels	bird sister	BRD SISTR
affricates	sounds such as /jr/ and /dr/; /tr/ and /ch/	drag chip	JRAG TRIP
intervocalic flaps	sounds made by double t's or d's	bottle riddle	BOTL RIDL

FIGURE 8.8

Sample Phase 4 Spellings

EGUL for eagle

BANGK for bank

MONSTUR for monster

STINGKS for stinks

TIPE for type

EIGHTEE for eighty

TAOD for toad

HUOSE for house

OPIN for open

ABUL for able

LASEE for lazy

RANE for rain

SAIL for sale

RIDDEL for riddle

BOS for boss

HOPP for hop

Look back at these samples and savor the fun and naturalness of their unique creation—every piece a treasure of the imagination of a small child who is growing into literacy in wonderment. Every child's journey is different and fascinating, but it's clear that their paths are the same. Figure 8.9 juxtaposes the samples of Paul, Meredith, Dan, and Leslie to show you the one clear path they all experienced in breaking the code.

FIGURE 8.9 Four Children Break the Code

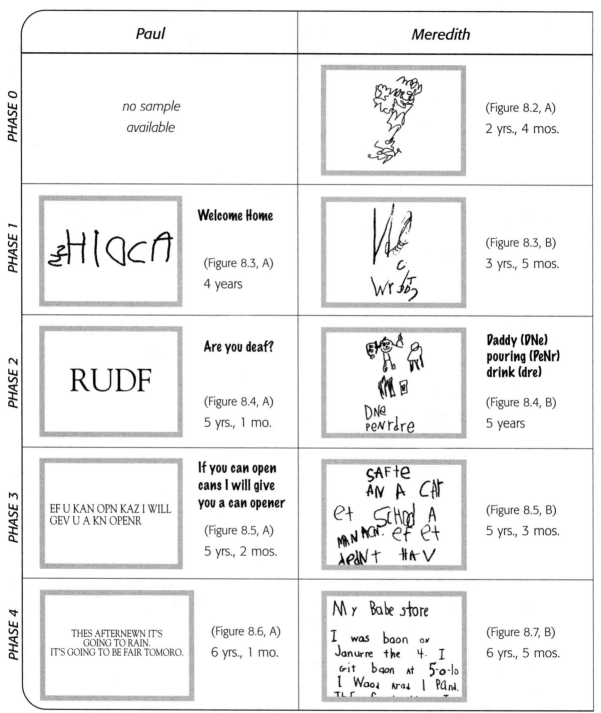

	Paul	Meredith
PHASE 0	*no sample available*	(Figure 8.2, A) 2 yrs., 4 mos.
PHASE 1	**Welcome Home** (Figure 8.3, A) 4 years	(Figure 8.3, B) 3 yrs., 5 mos.
PHASE 2	**Are you deaf?** (Figure 8.4, A) 5 yrs., 1 mo.	**Daddy (DNe) pouring (PeNr) drink (dre)** (Figure 8.4, B) 5 years
PHASE 3	**If you can open cans I will give you a can opener** (Figure 8.5, A) 5 yrs., 2 mos.	(Figure 8.5, B) 5 yrs., 3 mos.
PHASE 4	(Figure 8.6, A) 6 yrs., 1 mo.	(Figure 8.7, B) 6 yrs., 5 mos.

Dan	Leslie
no sample available	(Figure 8.2, D) 2 yrs., 6 mos.
	7Up, milk, Raisin Bran, doughnuts (Figure 8.3, C) 5 years
	A flock of butterflies (Figure 8.3, D) 3 years
	(Figure 8.4, C) February of Grade 1
	Humpty Dumpty (Figure 8.4, D) 6 years
	(Figure 8.5, C) March of Grade 1
	(Figure 8.5, D) 6 yrs., 3 mos.
	(Figure 8.7, C) May of Grade 1
	no sample available

CHAPTER 9

Fine-Tuning Phonics in Light of Phase Theory

Empirical investigations of how children's writing affects both phonics and reading growth may help phonics-first advocates refine theory and practice. Phonics and reading research should include investigations of children's early writing and observations of phase theory because beginning reading and writing or encoding and decoding are two sides of the same coin. Have neurologists fully considered that some of the brain areas activated for early meaningful writing from the child's imagination are likely the same areas activated for beginning reading? Will these considerations support the compatibility of code emphasis and reading-for-meaning practice?

In this chapter, we will examine important tenets of the phonics-first position obliquely by focusing on the work of one principal investigator rather than a diluted synthesis of numerous investigators. Drawing from the work of a single highly respected investigator allows for sharper focus and more direct analysis and critique.

Look at the following descriptions of code breaking from an ardent phonics advocate, Sally Shaywitz, M.D., a neuroscientist, professor of pediatrics at Yale, and codirector of the Yale Center for the Study of Learning and Attention, who conducted brain scans with dyslexics. Dr. Shaywitz is the author of *Overcoming Dyslexia: A New and Complete Science-Based Program for Reading Problems at Any Level* (2003).

One of the most exciting things to happen to your child between the time he enters kindergarten and the time he leaves the next spring is that he breaks the reading code. (p.178)

And then one day he solves the puzzle: He makes the critical insight that the written word sat *has the same number and sequence of sounds, "sss," "aaaa," "t," as the spoken word* sat *and that the letters represent these sounds. He has broken the reading code! The child has mastered the alphabetic principle. He is ready to read! (p.176)*

A position that espouses code breaking, even metaphorically, as something that just miraculously happens, runs counter to phase theory. There is no hop, skip, and jump from nonreading to proficient reading, with phonemic awareness somewhere in the middle. Does code breaking really happen in kindergarten for most children? No. But *Overcoming Dyslexia*, from which these quotes were extracted, might leave the reader with the belief that it does. Without a clear understanding of the when, where, and how code breaking occurs, we may bungle our help to the code breaker.

Phase theory presents code breaking as a step-by-step process that may extend through the first two years of schooling, though not so often "between the time he enters kindergarten and the time he leaves next spring." While some children break the code in kindergarten, they are usually the ones whose parents taught them a lot about reading and writing at home before they entered school. In all cases, I would argue, helping the child break the reading code involves more than Shaywitz's truncated interpretation. Defining code breaking as full phonemic awareness presents an incomplete picture that may lead to flawed curricula in preschool, kindergarten, and first grade—in particular curricula with too much emphasis on phonemic awareness alone.

Shaywitz's definition of code breaking—"*the critical insight that the written word* sat *has the same number of sounds . . . as the spoken word* sat *and that letters represent these sounds*" (p. 176)—matches a description of Phase 3: the child is operating with full phonemic awareness. While Phase 3 is important, helping children break the code involves equally critical insights coming before Phase 3, and after. Would this truncated view put all the eggs in one phonemic awareness basket and place too much emphasis on this one aspect of reading? Mastering the alphabetic principle is important; however, it is not the whole process, and saying that it is "the initial goal" may lead not only to unsuitable curricula but also to bad timing, inappropriate expectations, and bad policy in both teaching and assessment. Let's explore some of these risks in light of Shaywitz's recommendations.

From a phase-theory perspective, one might argue that the child Shaywitz believes has broken the code—who is "ready to read"—is simply ready for the next phase—that is, ready for chunking and learning more complicated insights into the code. Rather than occurring at the end of kindergarten, as reported by Shaywitz, this phase of development occurs in the first half of first grade for many children (Gentry, 2006; Snow, Burns, & Griffin, 1998). The child's first critical insight that printed *sat* and spoken "sat" have three letters and three sounds is likely accompanied with much pondering over the code and little clarity at having solved it. Without chunking knowledge, the child still doesn't entirely "get it." He must eventually relate *sat* to *bat, cat, hat, mat, rat,* and *fat* and construe the onset and rime parts, making analogies and substitutions with transformations involving *s-at* and *b-at*. Ultimately code breaking means stabilization and constancy with the CVC short-vowel *sat* spelling pattern. As Shaywitz herself points out, he must activate the "word form" area of the brain so that it fires off a particular constellation of neurons, allowing the child automatic recall of the word's meaning, sound, and spelling and eventually building an "exact neural replica of the word" (p. 189).

Shaywitz's description of the "Aha!" moment—the moment when the child "makes the critical insight that the written word has the same number and sequence of sounds, 'ssss,' 'aaaa,' 't,' as the spoken word *sat* and that the letters represent these sounds" doesn't account for creative spelling. At exactly the same time the child is first coming into the "ssss"-"aaaa"-"t" insight, she may spell *sat* as SOT or SIT because she doesn't know what letter makes the /ă/ sound even though she might decode it for reading. In some dialects, the letter name of two vowels, either *o* or *i*, may seem closer to the /ă/ sound than *a*, and closer in feeling in the mouth and in place of articulation. So while she's first decoding *sat* for reading, she might very well *encode* the word *sat* as SOT or SIT for writing. The *sat* epiphany described at the outset of Shaywitz's chapter entitled "Helping Your Child Break the Reading Code" may not be the essence of code breaking or the signal that the code-breaking challenge has been met. Nor does it signal "he is ready to read!" (p. 176) as he likely *already* "reads" pattern books quite joyfully with comprehension, fluency, and accuracy after a little repetition. A child coming into the "ssss"-"aaaa"-"t" insight likely can read the following:

One day Flora went to the zoo.

She looked at the giraffe and the giraffe looked back.

She looked at the panther with its coat of silky black.

She looked at the tiger and the tiger looked back.

She looked at the snake as it slithered through a crack.

(Fox, 1996, pp. 1–8)

He may even read partially decodable books:

Bob puts some popcorn in the pot.

He puts in a little.

He puts in a lot.

"POP" pops the popcorn.

Stop, Bob, stop!

The popcorn is popping over the top.

(Egan, 1996, pp. 2–5)

Yet he has not fully broken the code, for at the time of his *sat* epiphany his writing usually looks something like this (albeit with quite a few conventionally spelled words in the mix):

HEZ RITNG SOFEZTAKTD STORES

ABOT AL KIDS UF TOPX BOT D KOD

HEZ UZNG IZ A LITL KNFUZNG!

(He's writing sophisticated stories about all kinds of topics, but the code he's using is a little confusing!)

In this chapter, we will explore further ramifications of advancing a phonics-first position without the much-needed infusion of phase theory. We will look further at the time, place, and circumstance of code breaking and consider how and when the child breaks the code in light of Shaywitz's major recommendations.

Eight Expert Opinions That Should Be Reopened for Discussion

Shaywitz's recommendations are directed mainly to parents of dyslexics. However, any "New and Complete Science-Based Program for Reading Problems" should undergo close scrutiny vis-à-vis phase theory. Let's investigate eight of her statements or recommendations. Dr. Shaywitz's work is especially appropriate for this critical analysis because she is perhaps the most famous and influential of the phonics-first experts.

Is Sound Advice Sound Advice?

> At the very beginning stage of reading the initial goal is to draw the child's attention to the sounds of language.
>   (Shaywitz, 2003, p.177)

From a phase theory perspective, this statement is only partly accurate. There are many initial goals of equal importance at the very beginning of reading. The best way for the preschooler or kindergartner to understand concepts about sounds in language (for example, due to man's unconscious and automatic production of spoken language), may be to draw the child's attention to writing, rather than sounds without letters. In addition to attention to sounds, the child must be motivated and interested in the process. If the teacher asks the child to shout out the rhyming word in a nursery rhyme, for example, the poem itself must have meaning and significance in order for the child to have joy or interest in it. It's not enough just to draw attention to the sounds of the rhyme. Some preschool phonemic awareness programs, unfortunately, are boring and only remotely related to reading. Even though Shaywitz cautions against allowing phonemic awareness to become an end in itself, that's exactly what happens in some of these instructional programs: the "end" becomes a passing score on a phonemic awareness test or a tally of how many "items"—sounds or letters—the youngster can tag in one minute, and the joy of reading is lost!

Beyond that, what particular sounds does Shaywitz have in mind? Rhymes, syllables, onsets and rimes, phonemes, beginning sounds, middle sounds, ending sounds, vowel sounds, digraph sounds, diphthongs, any sounds at any time? For most teachers, the directive to "draw the child's attention to sounds" is far too ambiguous. Teachers need to know which sounds should be addressed at the beginning of reading and how.

Phase theory provides a clear statement of which sounds children must attend to at what time. At the very beginning stage of reading, the initial goal is to determine the child's phase, notice what the child pays attention to as a reader and writer, encourage the child to write and enjoy books, and offer precise guidance to get the child to the next level of attention in a step-by-step process. This includes appropriate attention to the particular levels of sound sophistication—rhymes, syllables, and the sounds in one's name in the initial phases, and more sophisticated sound work later.

Is Phonemic Awareness an End in Itself? How Does It Develop?

> The end point is for a child to develop phonemic awareness, the most important and sometimes most difficult task in learning to read and the foundation of all subsequent reading and spelling instruction . . . Always keep in mind that we are teaching phonemic awareness not as an end in itself, but because of its central importance in helping a child understand the relation of letters to sounds and ultimately, to become a reader.
>
> (Shaywitz, 2003, pp. 178–179, emphasis added)

Phonemic awareness, which Shaywitz (2003) defines as "the ability to notice, identify, and manipulate the individual sounds-phonemes-in spoken words" (p. 51), seems to cause a lot of confusion. Is it an end point or not? According to Shaywitz, exactly "how children develop phonemic awareness is currently not known" (p. 52), but from the perspective of phase theory, it's as simple as 1, 2, 3! You can clearly see how phonemic awareness developed in the case studies of Paul, Meredith, Dan, and Leslie presented in Chapter 8. It developed from no awareness at Phases 0 and 1 to partial awareness at Phase 2, to full awareness at Phase 3. When we look at what children pay attention to in early writing, the development of phonemic awareness is abundantly clear. It develops through experience with written and printed language, and one can clearly see its development in these children's writing. Since learning to speak is innate and not part of the child's consciousness, perhaps "writing first"—that is to say, early experience with *written* language—is the best way to make phonemic awareness concrete and make it pop in the child's brain. Observing the child's writing is the best way to test for the presence of phonemic awareness and letter knowledge and to determine the level of sophistication of their use.

Too frequently, assessments of early literacy development measure how many items the child knows. DIBELS, for example, is a well-known test that measures how many letters or sounds the child can identify in one minute. But this is like going to a junkyard and looking at parts. The parts can't do anything by themselves. Instead, we should look for the natural appearance of these items in the child's writing and his expected change in strategic operations while using these items both in writing and reading. What the phase theorist sees in children's writing and invented spelling is the tangible representation of the child's unified theory of how the whole reading/writing process works—not merely some part called "letter knowledge" or "phonemic awareness."

The development of phonemic awareness is critical to literacy. Perhaps one of the greatest contributions of Shaywitz's important work is her clarification of the role phonemic awareness plays in dyslexia. In her discussion of dyslexic readers, describing one patient named Alex, she writes, "A circumscribed, encapsulated deficit in phonologic processing interferes with Alex's decoding, preventing word identification. This basic weakness in what is essentially a lower-level language function blocks access to higher-order language processes and to gaining meaning from text" (53). In other words, Alex can't read because his phonemic awareness is impaired, yet his higher-order intellectual abilities and systems for comprehension and meaning are completely intact. Shaywitz's discovery of when, where, and how to deal with dyslexia, specifically with very early intervention in kindergarten and first grade, may be the secret to overcoming this debilitating condition. I believe attention to phase development will help clarify when and how to intervene.

When Do Children Learn Their Letters?

> Most children have already learned to sing the ABC song as preschoolers and enter kindergarten knowing the names of most letters. In kindergarten, knowledge of the letters is reinforced—not only their shapes and names but their sounds. By the second half of the year, most children can identify and print each of the letters. Now they can begin to use them for the purpose of reading.
>
> (Shaywitz, 2003, p.188)

Many kindergarten teachers would not find it amusing to learn that they are merely "reinforcing" the learning of letters in their classrooms. On the first day of school in 2006, as 55 million children enrolled in American schools, hundreds of thousands of America's kindergartners could not sing the ABC song. Many of them could not speak English. Over a million of them could not write their names. According to statistics released by the National Center for Education Statistics and Early Childhood Longitudinal Study Program, we can expect that about 1.5 million children did not know their letters when they entered America's kindergartens this year (West, Denton, & Germino-Hausken, 2000, pp. 22–24). And that is precisely the problem.

Shaywitz's description of the time, place, and circumstances of letter knowledge and letter writing applies only to privileged children in privileged America, perhaps the ones whose parents have the means to buy a book such as *Overcoming Dyslexia* or take their children to a university clinic for fMRI screening—most of those children *do* know the names of letters when they enter kindergarten, but the rest of America's children do not.

From my observation in poor rural America, in poor urban America, and in schools where a majority of the children speak a language other than English at home, about half of the children enter kindergarten unable to write their name. American education's lack of attention to closing the literacy gap *before* children enter kindergarten with universal preschool education is an egregious oversight. The children who enter kindergarten unable to write their name are the same ones who drop out of high school, victims of the high school "achievement gap" much lamented in the nation's No Child Left Behind Act. The next time you visit a kindergarten on the first day of school, ask the children of immigrants to sing the alphabet song. Ask them to write their name.

American education's lack of attention to closing the literacy gap before children enter kindergarten with universal preschool education is an egregious oversight.

::

What Is the Sequence of Code Breaking?

> *Once a child has learned about the segmental nature of spoken words and is becoming familiar with individual sounds, she is ready for letters.*
>
> (Shaywitz, 2003, p.188).

For me, Shaywitz's chapter in *Overcoming Dyslexia* entitled "Helping Your Child Break the Code" is difficult to follow because her sequence ignores the parallel development of several aspects of beginning literacy—knowledge of letters, sounds, book concepts, and reciprocal aspects of reading and writing that are all happening at the same time. In Part One of the chapter, the headings begin with

"Step One: Developing an Awareness for Rhyme," and then "Step Two: Working on Words," which includes "Separating Words into Syllables" and "Separating Syllables into Phonemes." The problem with Shaywitz's sequence, which draws from the work of Yopp and Yopp (2000) reported in this book on page 35, is that knowledge of letters, words, book concepts, and other aspects of reading and writing are all happening at the same time that children are learning about sounds. In the real world many children begin using letters to write their names even before they learn about the segmental nature of spoken words through rhyming, clapping syllables, or becoming familiar with individual sounds. In the real world a child is ready for letters as soon as she tries to write or read her name for the first time—she need not complete sound work before she is "ready for letters." In fact, learning to write her name puts the sound work and all the rest in context and may eventually make the teaching of sounds more concrete and easier to understand.

Part Two of Shaywitz's "Helping Your Child Break the Code" begins with the heading "The A to Z of Teaching Beginning Reading," with subheadings listed as follows though I have added the letters:

Part Two of the Code: Put It in Writing

The A to Z of Teaching Reading (p. 188)

A. Practice

B. Sight words

C. Writing

D. Spelling

E. Listening, playing, and imagining

F. Self-confidence

Following Shaywitz's sequence the child learns the sounds first, and then she is ready for letters, or "visible speech." From there, the teacher has the child practice, learn sight words, write, spell, listen, play, imagine, and develop self-confidence, but there is no guidance as to when one might do these things or at what level. The headings seem well and good, but without a clear focus or sequence, they are impossible to follow with exactitude. Teachers need a clear sequence for teaching sight words, writing, spelling, and all the others integrated into a comprehensive instructional program. By following the strategic operations beginning readers and writers acquire in a natural step by step progression and by allowing the phase sequence to help one determine the type and timing of instruction precisely, a teacher of reading can teach into the "real world" sequence of code breaking.

Do Words Have Patterns? Do They Follow the Rules?

Sometimes, however, difficulty arises where you might least expect it. I am thinking of words such as a, is, are, one, two, said, again, been, could, the, and once, which pop up frequently in books for young children but don't seem to follow the rules. These words do not follow a pattern and cannot be sounded out.

(Shaywitz, 2003, p.190)

Phase theorists sound out *all* words, including those on Shaywitz's list above. Some are sounded out with one letter, and some are sounded out in chunks. The notion that *words may be sounded out in chunks* is a fundamental phase-theory concept that every phonics advocate needs to understand. Once the code is finally broken *i-n-t-e-r-e-s-t-i-n-g* becomes *in-ter-est-ing* (Ehri, 1997) if it's being decoded by a reader for the first time. It's sounded out in chunks! In addition to believing that all words can be sounded out, phase theorists believe words may sometimes be sounded out in more than one way, which is easily demonstrated by different dialects. *Ate* is sounded out by attaching sound to one chunk of letters, and *eight* is sounded out by attaching sound to a different chunk. Both follow patterns—*ate, hate, fate, rate, eight, freight, weight,* and the like. No words are irregular in English—all make the same sound every time we see them—except for a few that make more than one sound, which we can't read out of context, such as *read*, which may sound like *red* or rhyme with *seed*. Phase theory recognizes that the code is regular and sometimes complex. Phase theorists are confused when phonics advocates say difficulty arises when decoding words such as *is*. *Is* helps me decode quite a few other words. Here are some *is* words that start with *a*:

Aaliis	abatis
abattis	abiogenesis
abiosis	abris
acariasis	acidosis

acropolis	actinomycosis
adenitis	adenohypophysis
adenosis	adiposis
Adonis	adzukis
aegis	aepyornis
aerobiosis	afghanis
agenesis	agoutis
agranulocytosis	

Phase theorists say that all words have patterns. Sometimes the patterns appear frequently and sometimes they do not. *Two* doesn't have a frequently used pattern, but it's easy to learn and it follows a hard-and-fast rule: "*T-w-o* is the spelling of the name for the numeral 2. *Two* always refers to the number and is pronounced /tü/, or like *tool* without the *l*. When *two* appears in a word and it's not the number, it makes other sounds, as in ba*two*man!" The spelling pattern for a particular word in a particular context with a particular meaning is always constant—except when words have more than one spelling such as *worshiping* and *worshipping*. I love the pattern and consistency of English spelling!

What About Invented Spelling?

Invented spelling functions as a transitional step as kindergartners try their hand at matching letters to sounds. When children try to form print words based on the sounds they hear in spoken words, it is a good indication that they are on the road to reading. This is why children in kindergarten and in the beginning of first grade are encouraged to practice "invented spelling" and to write a word as they think it sounds, such as knd *for* candy, hrs *for* horse *or* kt *for* cat. *As you can see by these examples, beginning readers commonly omit vowel sounds, so a child's invented spelling for the word* house *might well progress from* hs *to* hws *to* house. *Notice that the pronunciation of the invented spelling is very close to that of the intended word. A child may have the sounds down, but he may not have quite mastered the link between sound and letters. In kindergarten that's okay.*

(Shaywitz, 2003, p. 191)

From the phase theorist's perspective, it's okay for all children and even adults to have sounds down but to not quite have mastered the link between sound and letters because spelling is harder than reading. Inventing spelling is a fundamental aspect of breaking the code, and writing in invented spelling may be the best way to break it. When beginners write and invent spellings, the process is slow and analytical, as the beginner activates brain areas A and B (Shaywitz, 2003; Gentry, 2006). Inventing spelling fits the Vygotskian recommendation for materialization techniques: the process aligns a tangible object, the pen or the print, with a physical action, writing down the sounds or feeling them form in the mouth, and both the tangible object and the movement help the child represent a complex mental concept—the code (Bodrova and Leong, 1998; Galperin, 1969; Gentry, 2004). Early writing is concrete. The writer can see the spelling go down on the page as she is thinking of the sound she wishes to represent. This process makes inventing spelling the perfect vehicle for code breaking.

Early writing is concrete. The writer can see the spelling go down on the page as she is thinking of the sound she wishes to represent. This process makes inventing spelling the perfect vehicle for code breaking.

::

Shaywitz is mistaken to say, "Beginning readers commonly omit vowel sounds." They omit *middle* sounds. Beginning readers do very well inventing vowel sounds in certain contexts, illustrated in words such as *ate, eat, icicle, open,* and *united.* These words are spelled AT, ET, ICEKL, OPN, and UNITD at Phase 3 or likely A, E, I, O, and U at Phase 2.

Thirteen lines of text are not enough for a discussion of invented spelling in an important book such as *Overcoming Dyslexia,* or in any discussion of phonics and breaking the code. A deeper and more comprehensive understanding of the role invented spelling plays in early literacy development can enhance the phonics advocates' position by clarifying which phonics patterns are most needed and when.

How Does Speaking Vocabulary Influence Reading?

> *As a child encounters an unfamiliar printed word, he tries out different pronunciations: Is the i in ink pronounced like the i in ice or like the i in it? If he knows the meaning of the word ink, he is far more likely to pronounce it correctly.*

> (Shaywitz, 2003, p. 192)

From the phase theorist's perspective, the statement above is a bit convoluted. Of course the point that Shaywitz is trying to make is that children find it much easier to read words they have in their speaking vocabularies because they are mapping print onto their speech. That's why it is so important that English language learners, for example, know the meanings of English words if we expect them to read in English. On this point Shaywitz is entirely correct. However, it's not so likely that a child thinks to himself, "Is the *i* in *ink* pronounced like the *i* in *ice* or like the *i* in *it*?" What the child thinks depends on what he is paying attention to. In other words, it depends on what phase he is in. Linnea Ehri's empirical research in phase theory for sight word learning suggests that at Phase 1, the child doesn't even think about letters and sounds but uses some arbitrary clues to figure out the word. If the "ink" is environmental print on a label for Mom's computer cartridge, he may think, "That says 'Don't touch!'" because that's what Mommy says every time he touches it.

If the child is Phase 2, he may think, "*Ink* says 'ice,'" because he may only pay attention to the beginning letter, using partial phonemic awareness. Perhaps he already knows the word *ice* because he learned it from all those times his family went to the gas station to pick up *ice* and he saw *ice* on the ice machine and he saw *ice* on the bag. And Mommy joyfully told Daddy the first time Johnny read the word *ice*. At Phase 2 he might read *ink* as *ice* because even though he's cueing on spelling, he's working with very limited letter-sound information. One sees this phenomenon in Ehri's studies in which a Phase 2 reader sees a nonword such as *kug* and reads it as though it were a real word such as *king* (Ehri, 1997). The Phase 2 reader might also say *ice* for *ink* if he doesn't know the meaning of the word *ink* (as if *ink* were a nonword). Ehri (1992, 1997) found that readers in Phase 2 probably don't have enough memory for detail in words to be able to read words by analogy (unless they have the word family in view), so it is highly unlikely that the Phase 2 child would be thinking, "Is the *i* in *ink* pronounced like the *i* in *ice* or like the *i* in *it*?" At this phase the child has stabilized the concept that a printed word matches a spoken word and may soon realize that the middle part gives clues also (Morris et al., 2003).

At Phase 3 children are paying attention to all the letters in the word and can read more accurately than at the previous stage, and they are more successful at distinguishing among similarly spelled words (Ehri, 1998). They also begin to read new words by analogy to known words. So if our *ink* reader happens to know *pink*, instead of thinking "Is the *i* in *ink* pronounced like the *i* in *ice* or like the *i* in *it?*" he's probably thinking, "Oh, this word, *i-n-k*, is like *pink* without the /p/ sound. It must be *ink!*" Another possibility at Phase 3, which is closest to Shaywitz's example, is that the reader will simply sound it out letter by letter. That might have been a slow and analytical /ī/, /n/, /k/, which might trigger "ink" even though it isn't exactly the correct sequence of sounds, or it might have been—/ĭ/ , /n/, and /k/—resulting in *ink*. In neither case did he think of *it* or *ice*.

The Phase 4 reader is likely to attack this unfamiliar printed word in chunks. If he knows *pink*, as with the Phase 3 reader, he is likely to pay attention to the *ink* chunk and say "ink." Another possibility is that he will notice the *in* chunk, which he knows is *in*, and put a /k/ at the end: /in/, /k/. The only child who would ever think, "Is the *i* in *ink* pronounced like the *i* in *ice* or like the *i* in *it?*" is a child who has had too much phonics instruction and has been taught to look at words with tunnel vision, as opposed to the more natural phase-theory analysis. It's rare that the child would pronounce this word correctly simply because he knows what ink is.

Is There Scientific Evidence Supporting the Use of Adult Underwriting When Children Invent Spelling?

How about for writing workshop in kindergarten and for language experience approach (LEA) stories? Would these approaches be included in scientifically based reading programs? Would they qualify for funding?

> *Kindergarten children also love to make up stories and to dictate them to their teacher or to their parent, who magically transcribes each word onto paper. As a child dictates his little story and then watches as you point to and read each word back to him, he is learning to associate sound, letters, and meaning. He is building the integrated neural circuits necessary for reading. He is also building his imagination.* (Shaywitz, 2003, p. 193)

In this tiny section of *Overcoming Dyslexia*, Sally Shaywitz succinctly and brilliantly describes the whole beginning reading package—a technique and process in which the child expands his imagination and learns "to associate sound, letters, and meaning" as he builds "integrated neural circuits necessary for reading." It will be a sign of progress when phonics-first advocates pay more than lip service to this process. Those who profess to be standard bearers of the "evidence base" must be objective and comprehensive and more inclusive. When we know, as Shaywitz demonstrates in her statement above, that approaches such as "writing first" (integrating the use of adult underwriting and LEA with other evidence-based positions) work, we cannot pretend that a few phonics-first programs are the only solution to America's reading problems. We cannot institute a Reading First policy, as the federal government suggests, that excludes writing and reading back writing. Scientifically informed professional development funding for teachers must not be exclusionary—it must be comprehensive and include techniques such as the one Shaywitz describes above. It's time for Reading First guidelines to adopt Reading *and* Writing First!

Call to Action

The Twenty-First Century: Learning to Keep Learning

In 2006 *New York Times* Op-Ed columnist Thomas L. Friedman returned from an international education seminar in Beijing impressed with the Chinese approach to education. China plans to become an "innovation country" with a new national strategy investing in education, which will lead it "into the rank of innovation-oriented countries by 2020." Friedman mused over the question of whether China will dominate the twenty-first century—"Oh you know the line: Great Britain dominated the nineteenth century, America dominated the twentieth and now China is going to dominate the twenty-first. It's game over." He remarks further about China's impressive effort to end illiteracy and its increase in high school grads and universities. Then in a brilliant stroke of his pen, he gets to the meat of his column entitled "Learning to Keep Learning," quoting Marc Tucker, the head of America's own National Center on Education and the Economy:

> *One thing we know about creativity is that it typically occurs when people who have mastered two or more quite different fields use the framework in one to think afresh about the other, said Mr. Tucker, and he focuses on how to make that kind of thinking integral to every level of education.*
>
> *That means, he adds, revamping an education system designed in the 1900s for people to do "routine work," and refocusing it on producing people who can imagine things that have never been available before, who can create ingenious marketing and sales campaigns, write books, build*

furniture, make movies and design software "that will capture people's imaginations and become indispensable for millions."

That can't be done without higher levels of reading, writing, speaking, math, science, literature and the arts. We have no choice, argues Tucker, because we have entered an era in which "comfort with ideas and abstractions is the passport to a good job, in which creativity and innovation are the key to the good life" and in which the constant ability to learn how to learn will be the only security you have.

(Friedman, 2006, p. A-33)

The Friedman column is a clarion call. Indeed we do need to revamp an education system for beginning reading and writing designed in the 1900s. In the introduction of this book, I pointed out how my own doctoral program in reading education was grounded in the early-twentieth-century work of Edmund B. Huey, who pioneered many useful ideas but who also set the stage for the reading wars. I shared the humiliating story of how unprepared I was, as a beginning elementary school teacher, to teach beginning reading and writing.

Breakthrough in Beginning Reading and Writing is intended to chart a new course for beginning-reading and -writing instruction, one that will embrace "learning to keep learning." Like China, we Americans need to invest in education, and we need to innovate.

Neuroscience, educational theory, research, and practice have come together, clarifying more than ever before our understanding of beginning reading. Indeed we now know the developmental phases that all children go through in breaking the code. We can now pinpoint student needs and provide targeted reading instruction early enough so that virtually all children can learn to read and write successfully. I believe phase theory helps phonics-first and meaning-first adversaries find enough common ground to move forward. We must put reading wars in the past and redirect the politics of reading education toward the future. Educators, policy makers, citizens, and parents must move forward with guts and gumption to revamp beginning literacy instruction, so that all children will have greater access to literacy.

Three Proposals for the Twenty-First Century

Here are three innovative proposals for the twenty-first century for beginning reading education in America—and elsewhere where English is taught. These three proposals will help us learn to keep learning.

Innovation 1: Overhaul Teacher Preparation—With Special Emphasis on and Investment in Teaching Beginning Reading

Currently, there are flaws in our system of beginning-reading education. I call upon our profession to take action within our own ranks to overhaul teacher preparation with special focus on the teaching of beginning and struggling readers. I began this book with an admission that I was inadequately trained thirty-six years ago for teaching beginning reading. The training that most kindergarten, first-grade and second-grade teachers receive today is still inadequate. Many teachers currently teaching in kindergarten and first-grade classrooms have not been given the adequate support and professional development they need to be happy and successful in their first years in the classroom. Many have too many students and not enough core knowledge of beginning-reading and -writing instruction. They have had too little preservice and on-site mentoring and far too little on-site practice. They don't have a universal, well-defined core curriculum. Too many teachers face students who come to kindergarten underprepared for success with reading and writing. Kindergarten and first-grade teachers' pay is not commensurate with the importance of their work. They don't have status. The solution will require an investment and a change in national, state, and district policy. All teachers of beginning reading should receive training comparable to the training that Reading Recovery teachers receive today, and they should be among the best-paid teachers in the district, with salaries commensurate with those of principals and supervisors and with counterparts in other professions. It should be a privilege to teach beginning reading in America. The teachers who teach our children to write and read should be revered.

Upgrading teacher preparation and professional development in reading is tantamount to high-quality early childhood education. We need changes in both preservice and in-service preparation. According to a report released by the American Federation of Teachers in June of 1999, two million new teachers will be hired in the United States in the first decade of this century. How many of them will teach children to read and write? How many will be well prepared? Will research guide the profession in teacher preparation as recommended in the report? Will teacher educators "be conversant with the new research findings and incorporate them into their coursework in teacher preparation" (p.23)? Phase theory meets two of the report's criteria for the type of research needed to guide the profession: (1) phase theory provides converging findings from multiple studies and disciplines and, (2) phase theory can provide "core standards and a core curriculum," with specificity (pp. 23–24). It's not enough simply to call for innovation and research-based standards. The guidelines for teaching beginning reading and writing must be both comprehensive and specific, and we must have a well-defined core curriculum charting the path of code breaking. I believe the principles of phase theory outlined in this book provide a framework for moving forward.

In December 2006 I was working in a wonderful elementary school with my editors, other educators, and a videographer, interviewing beginning readers and writers who were in preschool, kindergarten, and first grade. Uma's interview was especially poignant. She was a six-year-old first grader who was off the charts as a reader. She wrote a wonderful story about India, beautifully illustrated and in almost perfect English spelling, with a sprinkling of Phase 4 inventions:

> India is where I
> come from. I think
> India is SPESIL. India even
> has gods with four arms!
> We pray to gods in the TEMPEL.
> They have lots of names. I love India
> because my grandma LIVSE there
> and she TELS GRATE STROYS!

I asked Uma how and when she learned to read and write so well for a child her age. She told me she learned to read at age 2: "My daddy taught me to point to the words and break them up into little pieces!" I complimented Uma and said that her dad had taught reading exactly the right way—that *he* should be a kindergarten teacher! "Oh no!" she exclaimed, seeming a little unsettled. "*He's* an engineer!"

Kindergarten and preschool teachers are as important as engineers. They should have the same status, level of education, and comparable pay. Furthermore, when parents aren't able to step up to the plate as Uma's parents did to jump-start their children's learning of literacy, America should provide preschools that fill in the gap.

Innovation 2: Provide Universal Preschool Access

Perhaps the only thing needed in America to implement this second innovation is to copy Great Britain's system. Getting right to the issue, Tamar Lewin of the *New York Times* (2006) reports "British's Labor government has leapt into the full agenda" of universal preschool programs—as have the governments of France,

Belgium, Italy, and the Scandinavian countries—while America has tarried for decades:

> Just a decade ago, when America's Head Start preschool program for low-income families was already 30 years old, Britain had nothing of the kind. But now, Sure Start, its version of Head Start, is expanding rapidly, while the United States government is considering budget cuts for Head Start.
>
> Other British efforts have whooshed past anything the United States has planned: A free part-time universal preschool program for 3- and 4-year-olds is in place in Britain and it is genuinely universal, with virtually all 4-year-olds and about 95 percent of 3-year-olds enrolled.
>
> The British are creating a system of extended 8 a.m.-to-6 p.m. schools, offering affordable child care for children 3 to 14, plus homework clubs, music lessons, sports and more. And since 1997, when the Labor government came in, Britain has created more than 1.2 million new child care places and adopted national day care standards, something lacking in the United States. (p. A-31)

Lewin's report weighs in on the research base:

> American advocacy groups, business executives and child care experts have for years been producing conferences, research papers and studies showing that investment in high-quality preschool programs more than pays its way—both during the school years, when it leads to fewer dropouts and special education referrals and more on-time high school graduation, and for years thereafter, when it leads to higher earning, lower rates of teenage pregnancy and fewer arrests. (p. A-31)

Lewin cites University of Chicago professor James J. Heckman, winner of the 2000 Nobel Prize in economics, who has found that "investments in preschool programs for disadvantaged children bring far higher returns than investments later in the life span, like reduced pupil-teacher ratios, job training, convict rehabilitation, or tuition subsidies."

Yet only about one in five American preschoolers attends public prekindergarten classes. Lewin reports that some states, like New York, have instituted universal prekindergarten, but that these programs aren't fully funded. Meanwhile, American business leaders overwhelmingly support access through parental choice to publicly funded prekindergarten. It seems abundantly apparent: America needs to invest in universal prekindergarten programs, and the time for this investment is long overdue.

Without question, as outlined in *Breakthrough in Beginning Reading and Writing*, preschool preparation has a direct impact on success with reading and writing. A recent study by Dr. Angela Fawcett of the University of Sheffield in Great Britain, for example, showed that small-group work with language-delayed preschoolers for as little as an hour a week for 10 weeks boosts skills more effectively than a year of remediation for 7-and-8-year-olds. But there is a flip side to the coin. In an era of high-stakes testing, it's as easy to be trapped by "too much, too soon" as by "not enough" (Tyre, 2006). This new problem, generated by our get-the-scores-at-any-cost mentality, has turned kindergartens in some over exuberant school districts into nightmares for young children—in one kindergarten in California, for instance, children were given a 130-word list to read. *Breakthrough in Beginning Reading and Writing* is designed to help avoid this trap by establishing the framework for more natural, kid-friendly assessments and a set of realistic expectations for early literacy and preschool development that will show the natural phases of breaking the code and help establish well-defined core standards and core curricula. Phase theory will help us avoid turning kindergarten into what Tyre calls the "new first grade" (p. 36).

Innovation 3: Create Incentives to Bring the Best Teachers Into the Worst Schools

In an article entitled "What It Takes to Make a Student," Paul Tough (2006) not only agrees with some of the policies mentioned above but champions an innovative addition: create incentives to bring the best teachers into the worst schools. The only thing I would add is that we need to create ways to bring the best *principals* to those schools as well. The gap between black and white or poor versus privileged children in America's public schools is accompanied by a teacher-quality gap. Teachers in public schools in more privileged communities in America receive higher pay, more status, and even better training than most teachers in poor urban and rural schools. This is despite the fact that their jobs are easier—not only do they have fewer students, but these students enter school better prepared for success than their poorer counterparts. The better teachers understandably flock to the better schools.

There is no shortage of research that demonstrates the need for skillful, well-trained, well-supported teachers to work with needy students (Darling-Hammond, 2000; Wenglinsky, 2000). But instead of bringing the best teachers to the worst schools, we do just the opposite. Linda Darling-Hammond and Barnett Berry (2006) call it "one of the most egregious injustices in the U.S. public school system: Poor students and those of color are the ones most likely to be taught by inexperienced and under-qualified teachers" (p.15). Beyond that, they report that the yearly turnover rate among teachers in poor schools is often around 30 percent. Darling-Hammond and Berry call for a national effort on the order of the post-World War II Marshall Plan—to recruit and retain the best teachers for the worst schools (p.16). Isn't that a splendid way to spend tax dollars and invest in America's future?

America must invest in education. A report by the American Federation of Teachers shows inadequate investment thus far: Teacher salary increases, for example, over the ten-year period from 1994 to 2004 (the latest statistics available) were far below other professions, with an increase of only $1,000 over that ten-year period (Aigner, 2006). We need bonus or incentive pay for teachers to teach in schools where the majority of the students are poor and underprepared for success in academia, and we need incentives to *keep* the best teachers in needy schools. Teachers' unions must have the moral fortitude to put the lives of needy children first and abandon harmful policies such as forced transfer rights, which can leave the worst teachers in needy schools by guaranteeing senior teachers the right to change schools whenever they want and bump better teachers out, even under objections from principals ("Bumping in Schools," 2006). A study in Illinois that ranked all teachers into four groups from "bad" to "best" found only 11 percent of the lowest ranking teachers in majority-white schools as compared with 88 percent in nonwhite schools. Only 1 percent of teachers in the highest-ranking group—considered the "best teachers" in Illinois—taught in schools where 90 percent of the children were poor (Tough, 2006). Our best teachers and principals are not where they are most needed, but with proper investment and incentive, this can change.

Are we Americans willing to make the innovation and investments needed? Are beginning-reading and -writing education important enough to merit these special considerations and effort? This book was written to prod you to think that they are. We need to transform how we think and what we do about teaching beginning reading and writing. We must learn to keep learning.

References

Adams, M. J. (1990). *Beginning to read: Thinking and learning about print.* Cambridge, MA: MIT Press.

Aigner, E. (2006, December 27). (Cited in Editorial "Bumping in Schools.") *The New York Times*, p. A24.

Bear, D., Invernizzi, M., Templeton, S., & Johnston, F. (2000). *Words their way.* Columbus, OH: Merrill/Prentice Hall.

Bissex, G. (1980). *GNYS at WRK: A child learns to write and read.* Cambridge, MA: Harvard University Press.

Bodrova, E., & Leong, D. J. (1998). Scaffolding emergent writing in the zone of proximal development. *Literacy Teaching and Learning, 3*(2), 1–18.

Bolton, F., & Snowball, D. (1993). *Ideas for spelling.* Portsmouth, NH: Heinemann.

Bosman, A. M. T., & Van Orden, G. C. (1997). Why spelling is more difficult than reading. In C. A. Perfetti, L. Rieben, & M. Fayol (Eds.), *Learning to spell* (pp. 173–194). London: Lawrence Erlbaum Associates.

Brown, J., & Morris, D. (2005). Meeting the needs of low spellers in a second-grade classroom. *Reading & Writing Quarterly, 21*(2), 165–184.

Bumping in schools [Editorial]. (2006, December 27). *The New York Times*, p. A26.

Burmeister, L. (1975). *Words—From print to meaning.* Reading, MA: Addison-Wesley.

Byrnes, J. P. (2001). *Minds, brains, and learning: Understanding the psychological and educational relevance of neuroscientific research.* New York: The Guilford Press.

Chall, J. S. (1967). *Learning to read: The great debate.* New York: McGraw-Hill.

Chomsky, C. (1971). Write first, read later. *Childhood Education 41,* 296–299.

Clay, M. (1982). *Observing young readers.* Exeter, NH: Heinemann.

Clay, M. (1991). *Becoming literate: The construction of inner control.* Auckland: Heinemann.

Clay, M. (1998). *By different paths to common outcomes.* York, Maine: Stenhouse.

Clay, M. (2001). *Change over time in children's literacy development.* Auckland: Heinemann.

Clay, M. (2005a). *Literacy lessons: Part one.* Portsmouth, NH: Heinemann.

Clay, M. (2005b). *Literacy lessons: Part two.* Portsmouth, NH: Heinemann

Clay, M. (2005c). *An observation survey of early literacy achievement.* Auckland: Heinemann.

Cooke, F. (1900). Article in *Elementary School Teacher.* (October, p. 111 ff.)

Cooke, F. (1904). Article in *Elementary School Teacher*. (April, p. 544 ff.)

Cunningham, P. (1995). *Phonics they use: Words for reading and writing*. New York: Harper Collins.

Cunningham, P., & Allington, R. (1994). *Classrooms that work: They can all read and write*. New York: Longman.

Darling-Hammond, L. (2000). Teacher quality and student achievement: A review of state policy evidence. *Education Policy Analysis Archives, 8*(1).

Darling-Hammond, L., & Berry, B. (2006). Highly qualified teachers of all. *Educational Leadership, 64*(3), 14–20.

Dillon, S. (2006, August 27). In schools across the U.S., the melting pot overflows. *The New York Times*, p. A1.

Dyson, A. (1988). Negotiations among multiple worlds: The time/space dimensions of young children's composing. *Research in the Teaching of English, 22*(4), 355–390.

Ed.gov. U. S. Department of Education. http://www.ed.gov/nclb/methods/whatworks/doing.html

Egan, B. (1996). *Pop pops the popcorn*. Parsippany, NJ: Modern Curriculum Press.

Ehri, L. C. (1992). Reconceptualizing the development of sight word reading and its relationship to recoding. In P. Gough, E. C. Ehri, & R. Treiman (Eds.), *Reading acquisition* (pp. 107–143). Hillsdale, NJ: Lawrence Erlbaum Associates.

Ehri, L. C. (1997). Learning to read and learning to spell are one and the same, almost. In C. A. Perfetti, L. Rieben, & M. Fayol (Eds.), *Learning to spell* (pp. 237–269). London: Lawrence Erlbaum Associates.

Ehri, L. C. (1998). Grapheme-phoneme knowledge is essential for learning to read words in English. In J. Metsala & L. Ehri (Eds.), *Word recognition in beginning literacy* (pp. 3–40). Mahwah, NJ: Lawrence Erlbaum Associates.

Ehri, L., & Robbins, C. (1992). Beginners need some decoding skills to read words by analogy. *Reading Research Quarterly, 27*, 12–26.

Feldgus, E. G., & Cardonick, I. (1999). *Kid writing: A systematic approach to phonics, journals, and writing workshop*. Bothell, WA: The Wright Group.

Fox, M. (1996). *Zoo-looking*. New York: Mondo Publishing.

Friedman, T. L. (2006, December 13). Learning to learn [Op-Ed]. *The New York Times*, p. A33.

Galperin, P.Y. (1969). The role of orientation in thought. *Soviet Psychology 18*(2): 113-134.

Graves, D. (1978). *Balance the basics: Let them write*. New York: Ford Foundation.

Graves, D. (1983). *Writing: Teachers and children at work*. Portsmouth, NH: Heinemann.

Gentry, J. R. (1977). *A study of the orthographic strategies of beginning readers*. (Doctoral dissertation, University of Virginia, 1977). Unpublished.

Gentry, J. R. (1982). An analysis of developmental spelling in GNYS at WRK. *The Reading Teacher, 36*, 192–200.

Gentry, J. R. (1985). You can analyze developmental spelling. *Teaching K–8, 15*, 44–45.

Gentry, J. R. (1987). *Spel ... is a four-letter word*. Portsmouth, NH: Heinemann.

Gentry, J. R. (1998). *The literacy map: Guiding children to where they need to be (4–6)*. New York: Mondo Publishing.

Gentry, J. R. (2000a). A retrospective on invented spelling and a look forward. *The Reading Teacher, 54*(3), 318–332.

Gentry, J. R. (2000b). *The literacy map: Guiding children to where they need to be (K–3)*. New York: Mondo Publishing.

Gentry, J. R. (2004). *The science of spelling: The explicit specifics that make great readers and writers (and spellers!)*. Portsmouth, NH: Heinemann.

Gentry, J. R. (2005). Instructional techniques for emerging writers and special needs students at kindergarten and grade 1 levels. *Reading and Writing Quarterly, 21*, 113–134.

Gentry, J. R. (2006). *Breaking the code: The new science of beginning reading and writing*. Portsmouth, NH: Heinemann.

Gentry, J. R. (2007a). *Assessing early literacy with Richard Gentry: Five phases, one simple test*. Portsmouth, NH: Heinemann.

Gentry, J. R. (2007b). *Spelling connections*. Columbus, OH: Zaner-Bloser.

Gentry, J. R., & Craddock, R. (2005). *Nursery rhyme time: Reading and learning sounds, letters, and words*. Honesdale, PA: Universal Publishing.

Gentry, J. R. & Gillet, J. (1993). *Teaching kids to spell*. Portsmouth, NH: Heinemann.

Gorman, C. (2003, July 28). The new science of dyslexia. *Time*, 52–59.

Goswami, U. (1996). *Rhyme and analogy: Teacher's guide*. New York: Oxford University Press.

Graves, D. H. (1978). *Balance the basics*. New York: Ford Foundation.

Henderson, E. H. (1990). *Teaching spelling* (2nd ed.). Boston: Houghton Mifflin.

Hoberman, M. A. (1978) *A House Is a House for Me*. New York: Viking.

Hoberman, M. A. (2007). A house is a house for me. In *Spelling connections: Poem and picture chart (kindergarten)*. Columbus, OH: Zaner-Bloser.

Holdaway, D. (1979). *The foundations of literacy*. Portsmouth, NH: Heinemann.

Huey, E. B. (1908). *The psychology and pedagogy of reading*. Cambridge, MA: The M.I.T. Press.

International Reading Association. (1998). Learning to read and write: developmentally appropriate practices. *The Reading Teacher, 52*, 193–214.

Lee, D., & Van Allen, R. (1963). *Learning to read through experience*. New York: Appleton-Centry-Crofts.

Lewin, T. (2006, January 11). The need to invest in young children. *The New York Times*, p. A31.

McGill-Franzen, A. (2006). *Kindergarten literacy: Matching assessment and instruction in kindergarten*. New York: Scholastic.

Mooney, M. E. (1990). *Reading to, with, and by children*. Katonah, NY: Richard C. Owen.

Morris, D. (1981). Concept of word: A developmental phenomenon in the beginning reading and writing process. *Language Arts, 58*, 659–668.

Morris, D., Bloodgood, J. W., Lomax, R. G., & Perney, J. 2003. Developmental steps in learning to read: A longitudinal study in kindergarten and first grade. *Reading Research Quarterly, 38*, 302–328.

Munsch, R. (1997). *Alligator baby*. New York: Scholastic.

National Institute of Child Health and Human Development. (2000). *Report of the National Reading Panel: Teaching children to read: An evidence-based assessment of the scientific research literature on reading and its implications for reading instruction* (NIH Publication No. 00-4769). Washington, DC: US Government Printing Office.

O'Neil, J. (2006, October 4). Early repairs in foundation for reading. *The New York Times*, p. A25.

Overbye, D. (2006, August 15). An elusive proof and its elusive power. *The New York Times*, p. D1.

Read, C. (1975). *Children's categorizations of speech sounds in English*. Urbana, IL: National Council of Teachers of English.

Read, C. (1986). *Children's creative spelling*. London: Routledge and Kegan Paul.

Rylant, C. (1996). *Henry and Mudge and the bedtime thumps*. New York: Simon & Schuster.

Schemo, D. J. (2006, August 3). U.S. issues new rules on schools and disability. *The New York Times*, p. A1.

Shaywitz, S. (2003). *Overcoming dyslexia*. New York: Knopf.

Silva, C., & Alver-Martins, M. (2002). Phonological skills and writing of presyllabic children. *Reading Research Quarterly*, *37*(4), 466–82.

Smith, F. (1973). *Psycholinguistics and reading*. New York: Holt, Rinehart, and Winston.

Snow, C., Burns, M. W., & Griffin, P. (1998). *Preventing reading difficulties in young children*. Washington, DC: National Academy Press.

Stauffer, R. (1980). *The language experience approach to teaching reading*. New York: Harper & Row.

Strickland, D. (1998). *Teaching phonics today: A primer for educators*. Newark, DE: International Reading Association.

Sulzby, E. (1985). Kindergartners as writers and readers. In M. Farr (Ed.), *Psychological bases for early education* (pp. 127–199). Norwood, NJ: Ablex.

Temple, C., Nathan, R., Temple, F., & Burris, N. (1993). The beginnings of writing (3rd Ed.). Boston, MA: Allyn & Bacon.

Templeton, S., & Bear, D. (Eds.). (1992). *Development of orthographic knowledge and the foundations of literacy: A memorial festschrift for Edmund H. Henderson*. Hillsdale, NJ: Lawrence Erlbaum Associates.

Tough, P. (2006, November 26). What it takes to make a student. *The New York Times Magazine*, 44.

Tyre, P. (2006, September 11). The new first grade: Too much too soon? *Newsweek*, 34–44.

Van Allen, R. (1976). *Language experiences in reading*. Chicago: Encyclopedia Britannica Press.

Wenglinsky, H., 2000. *How teaching matters: Bringing the classroom back into discussions of teacher quality*. Princeton, NJ: Educational Testing Service.

West, J., Denton, K., & Germino-Hausken, E. (2000). *America's kindergartens*. NCES2000-070. Washington, DC: NCES.

Wilde, S. (1992). *You kan red this! Spelling and punctuation for whole language classrooms, K–6*. Portsmouth, NH: Heinemann.

Wright, D. & Ehri, L. (2007). Beginners remember orthography when they learn to read words: The case of doubled letters. *Applied Psycholinguistics*, 28, 115–133.

Yopp, H. K., & Yopp, R. H. (2000). Supporting phonemic awareness development in the classroom. *The Reading Teacher*, *54*(2), 130–143.

Zutell, J. (1992). An integrated view of word knowledge: Correctional studies of the relationships among spelling, reading, and conceptual development. In S. Templeton & D. R. Bear (Eds.), *Development of orthographic knowledge and the foundations of literacy: A memorial festschrift for Edmund Henderson* (213–230). Hillsdale, NJ: Lawrence Erlbaum.

Zutell, J. (1999). Sorting it out through word sorts. In I. Fountas & G. S. Pinnell (Eds.), *Voices on word matters: Learning about phonics and spelling in the literacy classroom* (pp. 103–113). Portsmouth, NH: Heinemann.

Index